Nordic Noir

D0038387

www.pocketessentials.com

Also by Barry Forshaw from Pocket Essentials

Italian Cinema

Nordic Noir

The Pocket Essential Guide to Scandinavian Crime Fiction, Film & TV

BARRY FORSHAW

POCKET ESSENTIALS

First published in 2013 by Pocket Essentials,
an imprint of Oldcastle Books Ltd,
PO Box 394, Harpenden, Herts, AL5 1XJ
www.pocketessentials.com

Editor: Nick Rennison

A CIP catalogue record for this book is available from the British Library.

ISBN
978-1-84243-987-6 (print)
978-1-84243- 988-3 (epub)
978-1-84243- 989-0 (kindle)
978-1-84243-960-9 (pdf)

2 4 6 8 10 9 7 5 3 1

Typeset by Avocet Typeset, Chilton, Aylesbury, Bucks
in 9.25pt Univers Light
Printed in Great Britain by Clays Ltd, St Ives plc
For more about Crime Fiction go to www.crimetime.co.uk / @crimetime.uk

To all the Scandinavian authors, publishers, translators,
screenwriters, directors, producers and other creative personnel
who were so generous with their time (and company)
when I was writing this study.

Contents

Introduction

The Slow Explosion

How does one become an expert in a given subject? Scandinavian crime fiction and films, say. Hard work? Laser-sharp intellect? Knowing the right people? A command of multiple languages? In my case, becoming the UK's 'leading expert' in the field of Nordic crime fiction (I can use that phrase in all modesty, as it's not my quote) was, frankly, accidental. Writing about crime novels for a range of newspapers, and producing various books on the subject over the years (as well as editing *Crime Time* both in its magazine days and in its current online incarnation), it was inevitable that I reviewed as much foreign fiction in translation as I did the British and American varieties. (I always reviewed novels in translation – my expertise in foreign languages leaves a lot to be desired. Although, of course, I now speak perfect Danish after watching *The Killing*.) And I can clearly remember a time when the Swedish authors Henning Mankell and Sjöwall & Wahlöö were not regarded as part of any clearly defined 'Scandinavian wave'. They were simply highly accomplished practitioners of crime fiction, distinguished as much by their markedly left-wing perspective as by the fact that they were from a Nordic country (the former characteristic was by no means *de rigueur* in the genre at that time). But they coexisted alongside such non-British masters as the Belgian Georges Simenon and the Italian Andrea Camilleri – in other words, as very able writers from specific foreign countries, but not necessarily part of a wave. However, we can now see that these writers were laying the groundwork (albeit unconsciously) for an explosion that was about to detonate – an explosion called 'Stieg

9

Larsson'. When *The Girl with the Dragon Tattoo* was published in the UK (its title thankfully rejigged from the uningratiating *Men Who Hate Women*), we were aware that the author – already deceased before we had read a word he had written – was something of a phenomenon in his native Sweden.

But who knew we were looking at an all-conquering literary phenomenon?

No Crystal Ball

I'd like to say that I saw the current Scandinavian invasion coming, but, to be honest, I can't really claim any such precognitive powers. Along with everything from Chandler to Highsmith, I remember reading the influential novels of Sjöwall & Wahlöö and noting that this Scandinavian duo was clearly indebted to the American *87th Precinct* books by Ed McBain, and I also noted the remarkable pared-down, no-nonsense efficiency of the prose. What I confess I didn't notice was the Marxist perspective (more on that later), but the books ended up being salted away on my shelves alongside contemporaneous crime fiction from Britain and America and other points of the compass. The other major indicator that a Nordic literary invasion was on the horizon was, of course, the impact of Swedish writer Henning Mankell. (He was also influenced by Sjöwall & Wahlöö, as he told me – when speaking to other Scandinavian writers, I was to discover that virtually everyone in the Nordic Noir sphere was inspired by the duo.) Mankell's memorable Wallander novels, with their saturnine detective, quickly began to make a mark on the crime fiction scene – even becoming emblematic of the whole field. Scandinavian crime? Think Wallander.

The Late Mr Larsson

And sometime later, when *The Times* commissioned me to write a piece about the late Stieg Larsson (who was just beginning to create the seismic rumble that developed into the volcanic sales he subsequently enjoyed), it was clear that a distinctive genre – with its own parameters now visible – had arrived. However, this remained a literary phenomenon, and in the various pieces I was asked to pen I examined it simply in those terms. But then the second wave appeared, courtesy of film and television: the Swedish film of *The Girl with the Dragon Tattoo* and – on television – the amazing success of the Danish series *The Killing*. The latter went from cult phenomenon to minor British obsession (not least for its unsmiling heroine Sarah Lund, played by Sofie Gråbøl). And when in 2012 I found myself interviewing the modest writer of the series, Søren Sveistrup, in front of an audience enthralled by this talented (but hitherto unseen) creator, it seemed that the Scandinavian invasion was complete.

Happiness is a Thing Called Jo

Ian Rankin said in the *Daily Record* in 2012: 'Scandinavian crime writers are not better than Scottish ones, they just have better PR.' If he's right, Jo Nesbo has the best in the business. Perhaps the most forceful indicator of the current domination of the crime fiction scene by Scandinavians is the astonishing success of the Norwegian writer (and ex-footballer – and ex-rock star) Jo Nesbo. An indication of that success is the fact that the films of his work routinely precede the title with his name (e.g. *Jo Nesbo's Headhunters*). Until recently, the strapline on his paperbacks was 'The Next Stieg Larsson', a soubriquet which (I have to admit) was mine – except that it wasn't quite. I was trying to convey to newspaper readers that, if they had avidly consumed everything by Larsson, Mankell and co., they should try the remarkably talented Nesbo. But I can't really complain that my quote was tweaked slightly. Nesbo has since told me that, although his books are nothing like those of his late Swedish confrère, he didn't mind the quote... success is success. But even Jo Nesbo's celebrity represents only a fraction of the Nordic phenomenon – and the concomitant amount of remarkable Scandinavian crime writing now available in translation for English-speaking readers.

New Maps of Hell

This book is an attempt to map some of that territory, both on the page and on the large and small screen. Although every key name is here, *Nordic Noir* makes no claim to be absolutely comprehensive. I attempted that task in an earlier work, *Death in a Cold Climate*. Since that book was published, there have been many changes and developments on the scene. As well as providing a different perspective on some of the writers I have considered earlier, I include here some of the many compelling new talents (writers and filmmakers) who deserve attention. My aim? If I can send readers of this book out to a bookshop, checklist in hand, or have them pressing the 'pay now' tab on their computer, I will have done my job (though I must emphasise that I am not in the pay of the relevant publishers!). Over the years, I have managed to meet and interview nearly all the major (and most minor) practitioners of Scandinavian crime fiction, along with those very important (if neglected) individuals, the translators. This book is an attempt to cram all of that information into compact dimensions, along with the enthusiasm I feel for this genre. It's comforting to know that this enthusiasm is shared by an army of readers but, however well read you are in the Nordic Noir field, take it from me, there are new discoveries to be made. Myself? I make them every day.

1: Beginnings: Sjöwall & Wahlöö's Martin Beck Series

The Scandinavian Agatha Christie

There is no argument about it. Two writers started the Scandicrime boom, and remain the key influence on most of their successors: **Maj Sjöwall and Per Wahlöö**. But they were not the first. It is perhaps unfair to draw attention to the fact that one of the earlier writers in Swedish crime fiction, **Maria Lang** (her real name was Dagmar Langer and she died in 1991) was part of the old guard which younger crime writers felt the need to react against, despite the considerable success she enjoyed in her day with such books as *The Murderer Does Not Tell Lies Alone*, 1949. Lang's model was (unsurprisingly) the English 'Queen of Crime', Agatha Christie, and Lang was undoubtedly enjoyed by many readers because she presented a similarly unrealistic picture of her country, where crime is not the deeply destabilising force it is for later writers.

The First Stieg

Lang had been preceded by another important Nordic writer, **Stieg Trenter**, who also enjoyed great commercial success in his day, but Lang enjoyed a second readership in Great Britain, with her uncomplicated prose style echoing that of the creator of Jane Marple. Lang, however, was never quite accorded the respect and esteem granted to other foreign writers in translation such as Georges Simenon. The latter was quickly perceived to be an acute social commentator along with his status as a canny entertainer in his books featuring pipe-smoking inspector Jules Maigret. Lang's memory survives more than her influence, with many readers in the

Nordic countries cherishing fond memories of her books, avidly consumed in their youth. But after Sjöwall & Wahlöö, it seemed that there was to be no revisiting of the less confrontational, more comforting crime fiction of the Lang era – although, interestingly, the contemporary writer Camilla Läckberg has utilised Christie-like elements (notably the small-town murder) in her work.

Leading with the Left

While themselves avid consumers of the detective story form, Sjöwall & Wahlöö were nevertheless impatient with what they perceived as the bourgeois accoutrements of the genre. They became convinced that a radical shake-up (as adumbrated in the lean and efficient novels of the American writer Ed McBain, a clear inspiration) could benefit the form, by removing its more retrograde elements and allowing it to function as a laser-like, unsparing examination of society. And while the S and W approach was specifically Marxist, the duo were canny enough to realise that an undigested leavening of agitprop would hardly be conducive to their books having any kind of commercial success. Their approach (in this regard at least) was more indirect: painting a picture of a compromised, unequal society and pointing the reader in a direction which he or she might move to ameliorate it.

Hidden Agendas

One element of their then-innovative approach (now, like so many things in their work, overfamiliar from endless imitation) was the cold-eyed analysis of corruption within both the police force and various strata of society. (The corruption is at all levels – unlike, say, the English filmmaker Ken Loach, they did not posit an antithesis between unfeeling middle-class social institutions and essentially noble working people.) Those readers spotting the critique of the 'totalitarian' aspects of Western society may consider that the duo were discreetly closing their eyes (as so many did) to the reality of the application of Marxist politics in other countries where totalitarianism quickly – and inexorably – replaced optimistic ideals. Over the years they have been accused of naivety in their approach – the same accusations were later also levelled at Stieg Larsson, but more for his political activity than for the hidden agenda of his books. Interestingly, later writers have criticised the blinkered approach of left-wing thinkers towards the growing iniquities within the Soviet system. This is a motif to be found, for example, in the work of the Icelandic writer Arnaldur Indridason. But such considerations aside, *The Story of a Crime*, the collective title for ten perfectly formed books by Sjöwall & Wahlöö, hardly seems dated at all when read in the twenty-first century. The duo allowed their detective Martin Beck to investigate a variety of crimes which (in their range) cast a spotlight on many aspects of Scandinavian society. And the plot potentialities afforded the duo were considerable.

Not Just Sweden

It's not just Sweden. In recent years, the notion that Scandinavian crime fiction largely consisted of work produced in Sweden has been opened up and redefined, as non-Nordic countries (such as Britain) began slowly but surely to discern the differentiation between, say, Finland and Norway. But Sweden inevitably (and annoyingly for the other Nordic countries) remains the principal focus in terms of its market share – and the fact that the country is the largest geographically when measured against its Scandinavian neighbours. (It is, in fact, twice as big as Great Britain.)

Sjöwall & Wahlöö were well aware of the image fondly held by foreigners of Sweden: the intoxicating physical beauty of the country with its exquisite lakes and massive forests, along with a notion that Sweden represented the perfect encapsulation of the social democratic ideal. But S and W were keen to point out the cracks in this roseate picture and (along with such subsequent writers as Henning Mankell) began to draw attention to the social problems of their country, including such thorny issues as immigration. This is a recurrent theme in the genre – and a theme of particular concern to writers on the left who saw such issues as the difficulties of integrating immigrant populations into the host country as perfect fodder for the far right. Recent developments in the Scandinavian countries, such as the Breivik massacre in Norway in 2011, have perhaps suggested that the attention paid by left-wing crime writers to this worm in the bud of social democracy was, in fact, all too prescient. Significantly, the ideologically-inspired creators of the Martin Beck books had, perhaps without knowing it, lit a blue touch paper and the subsequent explosion was to bear the name of the writer Henning Mankell.

2: Sweden's Trojan Horse: Kurt Wallander

Wallander's Creator: Henning Mankell

Worldwide cultural domination of crime fiction by Scandinavian writers may finally have been achieved by the all-conquering success of Stieg Larsson and those who followed him. The groundwork for the Nordic Noir boom may have been laid down by the highly influential duo of Sjöwall & Wahlöö. However, there is one writer whose contribution can be called the most solid and far-reaching in terms of establishing the long-term popularity of the genre: the Swede **Henning Mankell**. The astringent vision of his country presented in his highly accomplished (and admirably consistent) series of books is not one that might initially have appealed to the Swedish tourist board. Mankell unflinchingly exposes the deep divisions in the society of that country, along with a variety of seemingly ineradicable social problems and the darker recesses of the psyches of his fellow countrymen and women. His copper, of course, is the troubled, middle-aged Kurt Wallander, the most celebrated of the fictional Scandinavian detectives, and the character's appeal is such that he has now been incarnated in a variety of TV series by no less than three actors: Rolf Lassgård (initially), Krister Henriksson, and, in a highly successful series made in Sweden but with British personnel, Kenneth Branagh. (All three series are discussed separately.)

Raising the Game

The series of Wallander books by Henning Mankell (now brought to a decisive end by their creator, as we shall see) is notable for a variety of elements, apart from its sheer readability: its impeccable plotting and nuanced characterisation (the latter as adroit as anything in the crime fiction genre), and its distinguished literary qualities. In the superlative translations by Laurie Thompson, the doyen of the translation field, the books have long enjoyed a keen literary reputation; like PD James, Mankell is frequently applauded for elevating the status of the once-disregarded crime novel into more rarefied realms. But perhaps the ingredient that is most crucial to the celebrity of the books is the infusion of the writer's own energetic social conscience, part and parcel of his desire to right the egregious wrongs of society. (Mankell's social conscience, like that of many another crime writer, has been shaped by the left-wing views of the 1960s. His political trajectory is in accord with that of many intellectuals born in the late 1940s.)

The issues addressed in the various books – from the corrupt influence of Big Pharma and the ruthless prerogatives of multinationals, to people trafficking and his country's barely disguised racism – are clearly powered by the author's own social engagement. (He is known for his theatre work in the continent in which he spends so much time, Africa, attempting to ameliorate the lot of ordinary Africans.) Surprisingly under-reported (in the context of the author's own activism) was the fact that he was present on the ships that attempted to break the Israeli blockade of the Gaza Strip. Quite simply, there is no gainsaying Mankell's dedication to changing people's lives for the better, as important to him as his literary activities. Readers, however, can be forgiven for preferring the time he spent on the latter discipline.

Breaking the Language Barrier

Crime fiction from a variety of foreign countries translated into English has long enjoyed a certain currency, but earlier writers such as Simenon were often regarded almost as British writers *manqués*; despite the clear disadvantage of being Belgian and having written in a language other than English. They had now been safely rendered into the language (it was felt) in which they clearly always belonged, by translators whose profile was far lower than that enjoyed by the profession today. Henning Mankell, however, was one of the writers who changed this ethos, not least because of the specifically Scandinavian tone of his work, markedly different in myriad ways from the kind of writing appearing in either Britain or America in the 1990s. The reviews for his first Kurt Wallander book, *Faceless Killers* (1991, appearing in the UK in 2000) were almost all favourable, remarking on a highly individual new voice in the genre, one whose writing had real heft and intelligence. Readers quickly took to the taciturn, difficult protagonist – not in the best of health, impatient, uncomfortable with his superiors (the latter, of course, being *de rigueur* for literary coppers) and struggling to cope with a variety of family issues. (As the series progressed, we saw Wallander attempting to cope with a father in the early stages of Alzheimer's and with a resentful daughter who felt neglected and betrayed by him.) But such was the richness of Wallander's characterisation – a richness shared with characters in many a more prestigious 'literary' novel – that Mankell quickly achieved pole position in the crime fiction genre. *Faceless Killers*, too, established the author's readiness to take on his country's fractious relationship with its then-undiscussed immigrant problem – and the non-assimilation of the incomers. In fact, it is a casually dropped observation by Wallander himself that throws suspicion on immigrants for the murder that launches the book – and although the detective passionately argues against fanning the flames of racism, he realises (in one of the very human moments that his creator frequently allows him) that there is, perhaps, a mote in his own eye in this regard.

The White Lioness (1998) is one of Mankell's most original and distinctive books, weighing in at a hefty 565 pages, but justifying its considerable length. A young housewife, well known for her work at the local Methodist church, has disappeared, and it falls to Kurt Wallander and his team to investigate. The detective quickly discovers that the events leading to the woman's disappearance have tendrils that stretch to far-away South Africa, and what comes to light is a tangled skein of malign human behaviour involving a murderous ex-KGB agent and renegade operatives of the South African Secret Service. What's more, the stakes are of the highest: nothing less than a plot to stop the rise to power of Nelson Mandela. Even before the reader reaches the epilogue, written by Henning Mankell in the Mozambique in which he spends so much time, *The White Lioness* (as will be apparent to even the most casual reader) is one of the writer's most political novels, with personal testimony and the experiences of people he has met in Africa having a radical effect on the text here. But as so often with the writer's work, there is no sense of a doctrinaire agenda at work – whatever else readers choose to take from the book in terms of what it says about developments in modern South Africa, the crucial imperative here remains the solving of the mystery by the implacable Kurt Wallander. And on the straightforward level of a page-turning narrative, the novel remains utterly persuasive – even though readers may fear that international terrorism, as pictured in the novel, has few limits and few boundaries.

Wallander = Mankell?

Mankell may not like it, but there are those who have drawn parallels between the saturnine Wallander and his serious-minded creator. That, however, is a congruence that he himself has always fought shy of. In such novels as *Sidetracked* (2000) and *Firewall* (2004), the reach extends beyond the memorable protagonist, dealing cogently with many of the key issues that affect Scandinavian society. Of course, one of the reasons that his books have had such resonance beyond the Nordic countries is that (despite their scene-specific qualities), Mankell – more than most writers of crime fiction – is well aware that we all live in what Marshall McLuhan once identified as the 'Global Village'. Many of the issues that transform society (for better or worse) are common to us all, such as the dangers inherent in cyberspace, one of the key themes in *Firewall*. In the latter novel, Wallander is actually used (ignoring for the moment his disputed qualities as a surrogate for the author) as a conduit into a world which for those of us who are not technophiles is *terra incognita*: we learn, along with the detective, just how our lives will be changed by the Internet.

Swedish Stereotypes

There are, of course, lazy stereotypes about the Swedes when it comes to the serious arts. (Let's leave Abba and football managers out of the discussion.) The Swedish intellectual is seen as a dyspeptic, over-philosophising soul, and the fact, now relatively well known, that Mankell was the son-in-law of the great Swedish director Ingmar Bergman (widely considered to be the most profound artist ever to work in the medium of film), lent itself to this kind of facile stereotyping. People were only too keen to say, in effect: 'Of course these books are bleak and downbeat – Mankell, Bergman's son-in-law, is keeping such gloomy philosophising in the family.' But leaving aside the fact that the intellectual underpinnings of the Wallander novels are richer and more complex than those to be found in most popular fiction, the basis for such an assertion is slim – serious though the books are, they are, in fact, told with a quiet storytelling panache that is utterly rigorous: the art that conceals art. For many readers, the tiny detonations set off in the reader's mind during the course of these books only become apparent some time after the reading.

Like many a creator, Mankell gave signs of wishing to move on from his signature character, and looked for ways in which he might usefully extend his fictional canvas. One of these involved the relatively brief use of Wallander's alienated daughter, Linda, now a policewoman herself, as protagonist in *Before the Frost* (2004). Here it was made clear that the detective's daughter was an example of the apple that did not fall far from the tree – Linda, unsurprisingly, turns out to be quite as bolshie and difficult as her father. Needless to say, *Before the Frost* was not received with quite the enthusiasm that had greeted the Wallander novels, but the reason Linda was sidelined as a character was not a result of this. It was because of the deep emotional impact that the suicide of the actress Johanna Sällström (who had so affectingly played Linda

Wallander in the Krister Henriksson TV series) had on Henning Mankell. He found himself unable to continue to write about the character. In the final Wallander book, Mankell's equivalent of a Reichenbach Falls termination for his hero was to bring about a sapping of his mental faculties (in much the same way that disease had affected the mind of the policeman's father), and the last book, *The Troubled Man* (2012) had a genuinely valedictory air. But Henning Mankell had already demonstrated that he had many more fish to fry in which Kurt Wallander was not to be involved.

Shadows beyond the Crime

Hard-core Mankell aficionados know – and appreciate the fact – that there is more to him than his crime novels. In interviews, the Swedish crime master is always eminently cordial and polite – but in the past, interviewers have learned to their cost that he expects his interlocutors to be well prepared. He is, however, patient with those who do not realise that his crime fiction is only one element of his output. 'There are countries,' he has said, smiling, 'where I am better known for my non-crime novels than my Wallander books.' And since Mankell has rendered his detective *hors de combat*, British readers are becoming familiar with a burgeoning strand of such non-crime books, including the remarkable *Italian Shoes*, in negotiation for filming by Kenneth Branagh, an actor who has already played Wallander.

The title of Mankell's recent book, *The Shadow Girls*, may suggest thriller material but it is nothing of the sort. (Perhaps the original title, wisely changed by the UK publishers, may have given a clue about the new direction. It was *Tea-bag*, the name of one of the characters.) In fact the novel – though involving – is a strange mélange of elements. The abandoning of a foundering ship near the beginning (with its black passengers left to their fate) is straight out of Conrad's *Lord Jim*, and the picture of the hopeless life of refugees in an unforgiving camp suggests that we are in for a sinewy drama channelling the author's own charity work in Africa. Here, we feel, is Mankell, the socially committed writer, addressing issues that really count for him as we meet a young black woman refugee, who describes herself as 'Tea-bag', who has convinced herself that Sweden is the place where she can start a new life. But like so many Africans smuggled into Europe, she is to find herself undervalued and despised.

However, just as we have decided we know precisely what kind of book we are reading, Mankell pulls a startling gear shift with the appearance of the barely successful poet Jesper Humlin. Suddenly, we find ourselves in the kind of literary comic novel colonised by such writers as Malcolm Bradbury and David Lodge, with a hapless Jesper henpecked by an impatient lover with a desperate desire to be impregnated, and by his short-tempered (and short-term-memory-impaired) mother who has an outrageous way of earning pin money. If that's not enough to make Jesper's life a misery, he has doubts about his own abilities, and his implacable agent bullies him into writing a crime novel as an alternative to his poorly-selling poetry. (Is Mankell, we wonder, paying off any personal debts with this strand?)

All of this is diverting stuff. Jesper even has a sparky Kingsley Amis/Philip Larkin-style relationship with another writer, with the duo enjoying dissing their colleagues ('it was part of their ritual to speak badly of the latest batch of new writers, especially if any of the debuting authors had been particularly praised.'). This isn't quite the kind of incisive comic writing that the British practitioners mastered, but the set pieces here are enjoyable. There is a disastrous poetry reading at which Jesper is verbally assaulted by immigrants who have been persuaded to attend – and it is at this point that Mankell pulls off a particularly smooth bit of legerdemain. Sitting in the audience at the reading is the luckless young woman we encountered at the beginning of the book – we realise that she has managed to get into Sweden. And she wants Jesper to tell her story.

The book's real agenda becomes clear. Via his unhappy poet, Mankell is giving a voice to those who do not possess one. We meet a fat and unattractive young woman from Iran (whose secure virtue is jealously guarded by her male relatives); another is from

Russia; and 'Tea-bag', although she has told people she is from Kurdistan, because she has heard that this will help her receive preferential treatment, is from Africa. These 'Shadow Girls' become the pupils of the reluctant Jesper in the writing workshops he finds himself bullied into giving. And, although he initially sees the girls as mere material to shoehorn into a future book, the immediacy of their lives soon brings about a seismic change in his own. Reading this unclassifiable novel, some may think wistfully of Mankell's Wallander – and even those predisposed to tackle different material from this writer may feel that there are two kinds of novel here, which remain obstinately heterogeneous. But such is the writer's skill that we find ourselves surrendering to whatever mode the book settles into at any given moment – and it might be argued that the comic sugaring of the social commitment pill in *The Shadow Girls* makes the novel's hidden agenda all the more potent.

Mankell Talks Wallander... and Other Things

The mice are a problem. Sitting in the lounge of an upscale West End hotel, surrounded by well-dressed couples sipping cocktails, the world's most influential living writer of Scandinavian crime fiction demonstrates the powers of observation of his saturnine detective Kurt Wallander: he has spotted that mice are scampering around the feet of the other guests in the lounge (a fact, fortunately, of which they appear to be unaware), and my conversation with him is interrupted several times by his bemused rodent spotting. Frankly, though, I don't care. As ever, speaking to Sweden's most distinguished crime novelist is a bracing and salutary experience, with so much more on board for discussion than the adventures of a much-loved (if dour) copper.

We are speaking a few days after Kenneth Branagh's pending knighthood has been announced, after a showing of the first episode of the new series featuring Branagh as Wallander (following Rolf Lassgård and Krister Henriksson). But, as ever with Mankell, the conversation ranges much further than the subject of his signature character. I ask about his new book, a standalone called

The Shadow Girls (Mankell aficionados know, sadly, that Wallander's police career – on the printed page at least – is no more). But writing something other than crime fiction is hardly a new initiative for Mankell, is it? What is the ratio of crime compared with other work on his writing CV? Mankell smiles.

'Of all the novels that I have written in my lifetime – that's some 43 or 44 – in fact, only 25 per cent could actually be called crime novels. For readers in certain countries, it comes as a surprise that I have written crime fiction. For readers in other countries, it comes as a surprise that I've actually written anything else! I have no complaints – it might be said that the crime fiction I've written has acted as a kind of locomotive, dragging the wagons of my other writing along behind. Such books as *Italian Shoes*.'

Isn't that shortly to be filmed? 'Well, Kenneth Branagh and I are discussing that. I'd really like him to do it.' Branagh's English-speaking incarnation of Wallander, while enjoying extremely healthy viewing figures (and a deal of critical acclaim) has not necessarily won over admirers of Krister Henriksson's Swedish take on the role. Ironically, though, when Rolf Lassgård's earlier performances in the role he actually created were finally shown out of sequence in this country, they were similarly found to be wanting when compared with those of Henriksson. Mankell, when asked in earlier interviews about which of the three actors he prefers, has always been studiously diplomatic. Can I finally draw him out, I wonder? I decide to give the contentious question another try – Mankell seems to be in a frank mood, and appears relaxed today (scurrying mice notwithstanding), signing autographs and pleased by the success of the new Wallander series. (The episode we've seen, 'An Event in Autumn', is based on one of his short stories.)

Here goes: which actor came closest to his vision of Wallander? Branagh, Henriksson or Lassgård? He frowns and muses for a second. 'Contrary to what you might think,' he replies, 'I don't actually find it a difficult question when I'm asked who I prefer playing my detective. You have to remember that I am a theatre director myself.' (Mankell, as mentioned earlier, does much theatre work in Africa, as part of his celebrated social commitment.) 'I'm also a playwright, and I spend a lot of time working with actors. So looking at the three actors you mentioned – Kenneth Branagh, Krister Henriksson and Rolf Lassgård – I'm not really in the position of having to pick a favourite. In fact, I don't actually think in those terms. I see the particular virtues – very different virtues – that each actor brings to the part, and find myself enjoying them individually, which makes the notion of choosing the best performer a touch redundant. All three actors – being very different kinds of men – bring something both individual and specific to each performance, so it's really not fence-sitting on my part to say that I'm impressed by things I find in all three.' He grins. 'I suppose that doesn't really answer your question, though, does it?'

It doesn't, but I know when I'm beaten. Nevertheless, I try one more salvo. Hadn't Mankell once said in an interview that his favourite Kurt Wallander was the first actor to play the role, Rolf Lassgård? 'Well, he was excellent in the role – in fact, I chose him. But when – for various reasons – his participation in the series ended, it was obviously crucial that someone equally accomplished take over the role, and it was at this point that I made it clear that I would like Krister Henriksson to be the new Wallander. In fact, what I actually said was this: unless we can have Krister playing the role, I'm not interested in any more episodes of the series being made. And – fortunately – I got my wish. Actually, I have the power that I need to have – I can choose directors, and so forth.'

I decide to try to probe Mankell concerning the controversy surrounding the Kenneth Branagh Wallander series. Despite a good degree of critical acclaim, there had been a groundswell of reaction against the show. British viewers showed themselves very much in favour of Krister Henriksson's performance and the qualities of the series in which he starred. The Swedish version was, for the most part, considered to be more authentic and closer to the novels. A judicious pause. 'Well, I don't really know what to say about that,' replies Mankell. 'The response has been different in a variety of countries. In Mozambique, where I have a home, the reaction was the exact reverse to the one you've just described in Britain – they consider the Kenneth Branagh series to be absolutely definitive, and preferred if to the Krister Henriksson. Frankly, as long as people are responding to one or other of the series, I'm not complaining. I'm very proud of all three series, and I'm always excited by the fact that they are strikingly different from each other.'

Although Mankell was present at the London showing of the first episode of the new Wallander series (written by Peter Harness after a short story by Mankell, and very ably directed by Toby Haynes), he had also watched it the day before in Sweden. I was struck by the arthouse style of the film: cool, existential and a considerable distance from the more direct and straightforward fashion of most British and American television programmes. Does Mankell consider that the influence of his late father-in-law is discernible in the series? 'Well, when your wife is the daughter of Ingmar Bergman, this is the sort of thing you discuss. When we both saw this episode yesterday, that very subject came up – it obviously struck you the way that it struck us. What we said was that if Ingmar had directed an episode of *Wallander* (and he did like crime films as much as he liked the kind of serious drama he was noted for), this might have been the approach that he would have taken. Principally, this would have involved letting the landscape and the silence interact with the characters – something that the director has tried to do here.'

This seems the perfect time to ask about the films that Mankell would watch in Bergman's private cinema. What did the two men view together? 'Well, Ingmar lived on a small private island to the north of Gotland. He had built himself a small cinema with 17 seats. This was a fully equipped cinema, and he could show the most ambitious films – in fact, he had his own projectionist. We watched over 100 films together – just the two of us – in that cinema. And what was as enjoyable for me as the experience of watching the films were the discussions I had with him afterwards.' So, I ask, would these be the kind of arthouse films for which Bergman himself was famous? Or popular mass-market films? 'Everything. Absolutely everything,' Mankell replies. 'For example, one day we might see a classic silent film, the next it might be the George Clooney version of *Ocean's Eleven*, before it opened in the cinema.

It was a wonderful variety!' Discussions on film between Sweden's greatest director and its greatest writer of crime fiction – surely, I suggest, that would make an interesting book? Mankell smiles. 'It's interesting that you should say that – in fact, I took notes of all those showings and discussions, and perhaps someday I will write it all up as a book. Certainly, it might change people's perceptions of Ingmar Bergman.' Journalists are streaming though the foyer, en route to a mass interview upstairs with Kenneth Branagh. But I think I've got the better deal – as Mankell imparts to me an observation which suggests the sombre approach to life of his father-in-law (and of course of the writer himself): 'You know, Ingmar said to me that when Fellini died this made him lonely, feeling that another of the great directors of his generation had died. But it was worse when Kurosawa died – Ingmar said to me that was the time he felt most keenly his own mortality.'

Of course, along with his skills as a crime writer, Mankell is well known for his keen social engagement, and somehow we get into a discussion of the year he was born: 1948. Talking about this date, he makes the kind of comment which suggests the provocative political beliefs that have informed both his crime fiction and his other work. 'Regarding the year of my birth, I'm acutely conscious of the fact that the nation of Israel was also born in 1948. Which means that one could say the problems of Palestine have existed as long as my own life. And I would like to feel that I will not die with those problems unresolved.' This comment naturally leads me to ask about Mankell's capture by Israeli troops when he took part in the flotilla attempting to break the Gaza blockade. Mankell wryly notes that when the news of his capture reached Sweden, a journalist phoned up his wife. 'At about 5am, Eva received a phone call from a journalist who said to her "Can you confirm that your husband is dead?"' He smiles again. 'She was… well, just a little upset!' I noticed that although Mankell later wrote a piece about his *contretemps* with Israeli soldiers for the *Guardian*, his participation (and arrest) had initially been curiously underreported – at least in Great Britain.

'It's a curious thing,' he replies, 'but I've noticed that some things are not actually reported in Britain. There is going to be a new flotilla, by the way.' Will Mankell himself be taking part this time? 'No, it would be useless. And I am now forbidden to enter Israel. I would not do the flotilla any favours by being present – it might be said that I would give the Israelis one reason to attack.' Did the Israeli soldiers know that they had among their captives one of the world's most celebrated writers? Mankell's expression is sardonic. 'Oh yes, you can be damn sure they knew. There were people there from army security to make sure that nothing happened to me.' Talk of such direct political action leads on to a discussion of Mankell's more political books – such as the controversial *The Man from Beijing*. Does he see himself writing more books in that vein, which tackle edgy world situations more directly? 'All I can say is that I will continue to write the kind of books that I myself want to read. And right now the stories that I want to read are those which have something significant to say about the times we're living in. But I don't think that makes me any different from some of my writing colleagues – take John le Carré, for instance. Look at the things he told us about the Cold War – and look at the fact that he is still writing these highly relevant, politically informed books today. In fact, we tackled some of the same issues – such as the influence of pharmaceutical companies, which was the subject of my book *Kennedy's Brain*.'

Of course, readers in this country are enjoying books by Henning Mankell courtesy of the excellent translator Laurie Thompson. I ask Mankell whether he discusses with Thompson the kind of book the next one will be. Do they talk about approaches and so forth? Mankell shakes his head and replies firmly: 'I don't need to. I absolutely don't need to – I trust him completely. My books are translated into so many languages, it would be impossible for me to check every one. But I do try to make a point of checking those languages that I *can* check – and it's only on one occasion that I have rejected a translation (it wasn't in England – it was in the United States). The language the book was in was not something that I recognised as mine.'

The mice are back, dashing past our feet – and, as before,

Mankell is the only one to spot them. He is bemused, pointing out that this is the sort of thing he expects when he is in Africa, but not at an expensive London hotel. This prompts me to ask how much time he spends in that continent. 'It depends what I'm doing, sometimes 60 per cent of the year, sometimes 40 per cent. I still do a lot of my theatre work – and I try to be ambitious. Recently I did a production of Ibsen's *Hedda Gabler*, and I made a specifically African version of it. In the text, Ibsen makes it clear that Hedda is the daughter of a general – so I made her the daughter of a general who took part in the liberation war against the Portuguese.'

I spot Mankell's publicist hovering expectantly in the doorway; it's time for a final question. According to Henning Mankell, what are the reasons for the current British obsession with all things Scandinavian – not least his own novels? 'Well, I suppose one reason might be that writers like myself brought something new to the genre. Agatha Christie, for instance, wrote a great many novels in which people simply kill for money – and I'm not underestimating her; she had a phenomenal skill at plotting, which one can only admire. But let's face it, character was not really her strong suit. Writers like me have tried to show that you can do something ambitious with the characterisation, as well as making your books be *about* something – and have something pertinent to say about the societies we live in. Actually, you can find something of the latter quality in Conan Doyle, who is still a big favourite of mine – I'm not sure that you English esteem him as highly as you should. For a writer, he is a godsend – you can steal quite a lot from him. Which I have done over the years. But back to your question: I think Scandinavian writers are as concerned with a provocative discussion of the problems of society as they are with the details of a crime investigation; that's perhaps what we have most contributed to the genre. A pretty good contribution, don't you think?'

3: Lisbeth Salander's Legacy

Personally, I've taken a certain pride in collecting Scandinavian scalps – metaphorically (with a handshake) rather than bloodily (with the flourish of a knife). I've assiduously tried to meet and talk to all the Nordic novelists I've written about over the years. Sometimes the meetings have been on their visits to the UK. They nearly always come to London, and friendly contacts in the Scandi embassies ensure that I'm invited to the various receptions that are given. Their publishers are also usually keen for them to meet friendly writers such as myself. Those who don't make it to London, I've tried to encounter in their own countries over a glass of wine or aquavit.

However, unsurprisingly, one Scandinavian writer I did not succeed in meeting on my multi-country odysseys was the late **Stieg Larsson** – still the most commercially successful of Scandinavian crime writers. (Although the Norwegian Jo Nesbo has now firmly grabbed the throne Larsson vacated. Nesbo's books have had phenomenal sales – one book every 23 seconds according to his publisher, Harvill Secker – and he has had enormous successes recently such as *The Snowman*, soon to be filmed by Martin Scorsese). But Stieg – and *The Girl with the Dragon Tattoo* – are still the best-known examples of Nordic Noir. The Nazi-baiting, chain-smoking author may no longer be with us, but his ex-partner, the equally feisty Eva Gabrielsson, most definitely is. Her memoir, *Stieg and Me* (published by Weidenfeld & Nicolson) pulled no punches. After much preliminary speculation over its contents, Gabrielsson's fascinating and quirky memoir about her life with the most successful Scandinavian crime writer of all time turned out to be a truly fascinating read. Gabrielsson ruled out no areas for discussion (including the now-famous feud with her late partner's family), but she delivered a book in which the single most striking facet is her love for her life partner who sadly did not live to see the success (or the posthumous furore) that the three books of the *Millennium* Trilogy caused.

Who was Stieg Larsson?

Few authors become bona fide phenomena in terms of unprecedented success. JK Rowling has achieved that status for her children's books, and more recently EL James has done something similar with her controversial erotic trilogy. In terms of Scandinavian crime fiction, one name, however, reigns supreme – and, ironically, it is that of a writer who would never live to enjoy his immense commercial success, the Swedish journalist-cum-novelist Stieg Larsson. In the crime fiction field, the American Dan Brown's worldwide sales – prodigious in the extreme – gave an indication of the possibilities for tapping into a readership that barely touched books. However, Brown's success (like that of the aforementioned EL James) came with a codicil that neither writer would have welcomed: a thoroughgoing, scathing dismissal of their literary skills. These were usually regarded as rudimentary, however many millions purchased their books. This scorn, of course, comes from readers who consider themselves appreciative of overtly 'skilful' writers, rather than wordsmiths more interested in keeping their readers turning the pages. Such dismissals, it should be said, are obliged to ignore the fact that these supposedly maladroit writers are able to hold the attention of millions of readers – as did Stieg Larsson, the creator of the laser-sharp heroine Lisbeth Salander.

Crusader to Entertainer

When I was commissioned to write the first biography of Stieg Larsson (*The Man Who Left Too Soon: The Life and Works of Stieg Larsson*), evidence of the Swedish author's astonishing domination of the crime fiction market was already beginning to emerge, although the sheer scale of his posthumous achievement was yet to be discerned. Who could have predicted that? Speaking to a variety of people (crime writers, translators, publishers and those who knew and worked with Stieg), I began to appreciate a startling dichotomy. As a writer, Larsson inspired total adoration from his readers and many people's relationship to the *Millennium* trilogy almost amounted to an obsession. Over and over again, I encountered people who had consumed all three weighty novels (*The Girl with the Dragon Tattoo*, *The Girl Who Played with Fire* and *The Girl Who Kicked the Hornet's Nest*) in speedy succession, utterly in thrall to the author's formidable storytelling skills. But there was another side to the coin. I also encountered those who reluctantly admitted that they regarded him as massively overrated. Yes, he was a hypnotic storyteller, but he was one given to wordiness and clumsy writing, with a sore need of editing. (It had already become something of a cliché that Larsson died before he had enjoyed a thorough editing process – a view contradicted by his Swedish editor, Eva Gedin, in a panel I did with her at the Swedish ambassador's residence.) In fact, one prominent crime writer (who shall remain nameless) took something of an axe to Larsson's reputation, but later (in the cold light of day) asked me not to use the scabrous views expressed to me as it would seem like 'sour grapes from a less successful author'. (It should be noted that this was a very successful author indeed – but few people could match Larsson in terms of his global conquest of readers.) Such was the strict division between those utterly given over to the Larsson cult and those with a passionate resistance to it. Why was this? I found myself examining my own feelings – and found that they somehow encompassed both extremes.

Contentious Elements

What are the most important elements in Larsson's success? Well, one might start with his very individual use of the crime thriller format, utilising its familiar tropes but forging an authorial style that was very much his own; or with the fact that he had produced these three substantial books before his death at the age of 50 – an achievement that can barely be overestimated, given that success in the field of commercial fiction is so difficult to attain (although Larsson seems to have had few doubts it was not beyond his talents); or the fact that the author died under what appeared initially to be mysterious circumstances. His now-famous work as an investigative journalist, specialising in exposing the strategies of the far right, led people to speculate that the brutal enemies he had made while working for the magazine *Expo* (in his fiction the journal *Millennium*, which his discredited journalist hero Mikael Blomkvist works on) had something to do with his death. And the final factor in this intriguing mix was the bitter dispute over the rights to his estate which continues to this day. His partner of several decades, Eva Gabrielsson, is generally considered to have been poorly treated and deprived of intellectual and monetary rights in his work which many felt to be her due. Although, needless to say, the situation (which until recently appeared to throw up some new revelation or point of interest on an almost weekly basis) is exceedingly complicated, and the heroes and villains are not as easily identified as might be expected.

Salander and Sexual Abuse

However, there is no doubt that one of the most contentious elements in the three *Millennium* novels is the graphic, unsparing treatment of sexual abuse. Lisbeth Salander, the author's memorably tattooed Goth heroine (possessor of the eponymous Dragon Tattoo), is repeatedly raped and abused throughout the novel sequence – and on one startling occasion, we find that we are reading a flashback to an earlier example of Lisbeth's desperate sexual history. The author's own feminist credentials are (it might be argued) beyond question; there are many superscriptions spread throughout the books detailing the grotesque abuse of women by the male sex (the original title of the first book was, tendentiously, *Men Who Hate Women*), and Larsson made no secret of his dislike of the treatment of women in fundamentalist theocracies. So did this passionately-held view (as the writer's supporters attest) grant his treatment of the subject authenticity and responsibility of attitude? Not everyone is convinced. Apart from anything else, we are virtually invited to cheer when Lisbeth Salander avenges herself on those who have sexually molested her. These include her abusive, corrupt guardian who pays for his brutal assault with a tattoo on his stomach describing him as a 'pig and a rapist' (one Salander makes sure that he is unable to remove), and also suffers the painful rectal insertion of a dildo to repay him for the anal rape he exacted on her.

There are many (including the British writer NJ Cooper) who do not feel that Larsson has earned this license, given the unrelenting and graphic nature of the rape and abuse within the book. When I first met the author's father and brother in London, the former told me that he had complained to his late son that the manuscript he had read was 'too full of sex' – only to be told by Stieg that sex was a commercial ingredient which sold books. And there is no doubt that the writer always saw himself forging a career as a popular commercial writer along the lines of those novelists he admired, such as Sara Paretsky in the United States and Val McDermid in the UK. The latter novelist, in fact, is name-checked in the books – she is a writer that Mikael Blomkvist settles down to read – and, perhaps unsurprisingly, McDermid herself has repeatedly been criticised, despite her gender, for a similarly frank treatment of sexual crime. (It's clear that she is tired of having to defend her record on the subject.)

Secret Identities

The narrative of the first book in the sequence, *The Girl with the Dragon Tattoo*, is now familiar both from the book itself and from the two creditable film versions, one Swedish and one American. Disgraced journalist Mikael Blomkvist is hired by a sympathetic elderly industrialist to find out what happened to the latter's niece, who vanished on an isolated island (the isolated setting a nod to Agatha Christie, another one of Larsson's favourite writers), and is presumed to be dead. Blomkvist finds himself relying on the reluctant aid of a damaged, vulnerable computer hacker, Lisbeth Salander, who despite appearing to be a magnet for a variety of sexual assaults, turns out to be phenomenally talented in a variety of ways. Her sociopathic condition (possibly a variation of Asperger's syndrome, possibly a result of her appalling personal history) is counterpointed by her super-intelligence, and she is almost supernaturally gifted when it comes to the vagaries of the Internet. What's more, despite her elfin appearance, she is also capable of massive violence, even holding her own against some Bond-style villains who appear later in the sequence. Her status as a superheroine is further enhanced by the fact that she appears to possess the capacity for secret identities, and is able to physically transform herself by removing all her Goth accoutrements and donning a wig. In the second and third book (after the resolution of the mystery in the first), her own story moves centre-stage, and a violent and titanic struggle begins with a series of truly appalling men (some even members of Lisbeth's own loathsome family), taking in the fractious relationship between the middle-aged journalist and his younger aide. Their sexual relationship is not to be a long-lasting one, but the accommodation that the couple finally arrive at is movingly handled by the author.

Reputations

When the first translation of the book appeared in the UK (by Reg Keeland, aka Steven Murray), the assumption was that this was a literary thriller along the lines of Peter Høeg's *Miss Smilla's Feeling for Snow*. After all, the British publisher was Christopher MacLehose, long noted for the elegantly written and extremely literary novels in the various lists he worked on – including the Peter Høeg title. But even a cursory examination of the text proves that this is not really the case. The prose here is (generally speaking) utilitarian, absolutely at the service of delivering a weighty and information-heavy thriller with the kind of closely-organised detail that had been finessed by the English writer Frederick Forsyth in

The Day of the Jackal. A lengthy description of the financial scam which destroyed the journalist Blomkvist's reputation is, for instance, given in exhaustive detail in the novel – but it is wisely dispensed with in both film versions. However, even Larsson's dissenters – and they are many – cannot argue with the storytelling acumen that Larsson demonstrates throughout his baggy but utterly compelling trilogy. Perhaps the first book remains the author's signal achievement, but the personal ingredients added in books two and three (in which we meet Salander's murderous relatives) raise the stakes in the most compelling fashion, and Larsson shows that, had he lived, he would have had the capacity for a very variegated career as a writer.

Disputes

The posthumous dispute over Larsson's estate (he died intestate and his partner has claimed that she was denied any kind of intellectual control over the product she worked on so closely with Larsson) has certainly been an unedifying spectacle, but it is something of a distraction in terms of the Larsson phenomenon. There is no question that the engine for Larsson's creativity was fuelled by the elements that engaged him on a personal level which included the insidious influence of the far right (neo-Nazis are at the heart of the first book in the sequence), and his horror at the treatment of women by his own sex. No male-despising feminist writer of the 1970s – when misandry looked as if it might replace misogyny as a cultural phenomenon – could have painted a bleaker picture of the male sexual impulse. When I spoke to the composer Jacob Groth, who worked on the Swedish film of *The Girl with the Dragon Tattoo*, he told me that male members of the cast were feeling an almost physical personal guilt at the scenarios they were obliged to enact in the service of Larsson's narrative. Certainly, most of the males we encounter are pathetic specimens, but we are able to identify with the good, positive exceptions to the rule, notably Mikael Blomkvist and the sympathetic industrialist Vanger.

Such considerations aside, however, the real achievement of the book is the creation of the astonishing female protagonist Lisbeth Salander, possibly the single most distinctive female character in modern crime fiction. There is much speculation over the fourth, unpublished book in the sequence (the author originally planned ten), which exists in fragmentary form on a much-disputed laptop, but it's hard to see how Larsson would have continued treating the traumatised Salander. The sort-of-peace that she acquires at the end of the third book would have to be ripped painfully away to establish the original dynamic in any fourth adventure. If that didn't happen, she would be just another tenacious heroine – and there are hundreds of those. But if Larsson subjected Lisbeth to cruelty once again in order to re-establish her as a driven, damaged avenger, he would have been guilty of as much cruelty as any of the unspeakable male characters who molest her throughout the books. We have the completed *Millennium* trilogy – and surely it is best that it is a trilogy, with something of a sense of closure, rather than an open-ended series of adventures, endlessly renewable, as in the case of James Bond?

The worldwide success of Larsson's work, which includes three of the most remarkable bestselling crime novels ever written, remains a singular phenomenon. His sociopathic Goth heroine and the caustic examination of the Swedish dream in Larsson's world of massive governmental corruption and sexual abuse had a seismic impact on the world of popular fiction. The American crime fiction expert Peter Rozovsky (who writes for the *Philadelphia Inquirer*) has posited the existence of a school of Nordic crime writing called 'Stieg Larssonism' (its practitioners are Larssonists) that 'combines potboiler thrills and righteous anger in a fat, sprawling tosh-filled package, often with 475 or more pages plus a didactic, statistics-filled epilogue in case the reader doesn't get the point – or in case he or she thinks the point was just to have some fun. That way the reader gets dirty thrills but feels morally uplifted at the same time.' Rozovsky had encountered a comment by Alexandra Coelho Ahndoril, the female half of the couple that writes as Lars Kepler, that Stieg Larsson had revitalised crime fiction and that the *Lars* part of their pen name was a tribute to him. (This is perhaps a cue for me to mention a book by the portmanteau writer who is **Lars Kepler**. *The Hypnotist* (2011) was a weighty and authoritative offering, with the murder of an entire family investigated by the intuitive Inspector Joona Linna. Linna enlists the aid of Erik Bark, a retired hypnotist, to work with a young survivor of the slaughter and his involvement proves to be shocking and surprising. The novel is an intense experience which justifies its considerable length.)

4: Larsson's Rivals

For a rounded picture, it is crucial to look at the growing army of Scandinavian crime writers such as **Camilla Läckberg** (a celebrity of JK Rowling proportions in Sweden) and sometime-London-based Swedish writer **Håkan Nesser**. Both offer a different perspective from Larsson. So too do the duo of criminologist and ex-criminal, **Roslund and Hellström**. This acerbic team of writers first encountered each other at a criminal rehabilitation centre and their joint creation, Ewert Grens, is a Stockholm cop. *Cell 8* is a typically scabrous example of their work. And there are a host of other provocative writers in Sweden, not least the distaff Larsson, **Åsa Larsson** (preferred by many to her male namesake). To some degree, the amazing success of the Scandinavian crime fiction genre is due to a perception that (rightly or wrongly) translated crime writing possesses more of a literary cachet than that written in English. There is a degree of truth in this, of course, but it is also something of a canard. As the Swedish writer Håkan Nesser has pointed out, it is mostly the best crime fiction in Scandinavia that is picked up for translation after a careful selection process by English and American publishers. 'You don't get to see the crap,' he told me, 'and we have more than our fair share of that!' The other perception, of course, is that such fiction affords a sometimes radical critique of the problems of society. (It's Nordic society in these books, of course, but by extension, the criticism applies to most of Western society – the genre somehow contrives to be both geographically specific and universal in its application.) If there appears to be more attention paid to the nuances of language in such books, that may be often due to the skills of the translators – and more than one Scandinavian crime writer has said to me that the work has been improved in the British edition over its original incarnation.

Bloodcurdling Cosiness: Camilla Läckberg

The bookshops of the Scandinavian countries and Germany are groaning under the weight of books by Swedish Crime Queen **Camilla Läckberg**, their windows festooned with her glamorous image (Läckberg is something of a gift to her publishers' photographers), and the tabloids full of discussions of her private life with her equally attractive husband. That dizzying level of celebrity is yet to be matched in the UK, despite the very best efforts of her British publisher HarperCollins. That's not to say that Läckberg is not popular in Britain and (generally speaking) she gleans a bushel of approving reviews for each new book. But there is no question that her breakthrough – in the kind of terms she already enjoys on the continent and might reasonably expect elsewhere – is yet to happen in the UK. And the reasons for this are a touch mysterious.

Is it because her literary skills don't suit? Not at all – she is an adroit practitioner of the crime novel, able to conjure a specific fictional world which is both persuasive and smoothly integrated. Characterisation lacking, perhaps? Definitely not. Again, Läckberg shows real authority in sustaining the protagonists she has chosen to use in her fiction, the writer Erica Falck and the policeman with whom Falck has a relationship, Patrick Hedström. Problems with locale and setting? Again, no: this area is one of the writer's most valuable weapons in her armoury. Her chosen town of Fjällbacka is one of the most perfectly realised settings in crime fiction from any country, with both the geographical and societal elements full of verisimilitude. It is a small town, and Läckberg told me that she is most comfortable describing such a locale (Fjällbacka is actually her hometown) rather than a more cosmopolitan, less insular setting. Her location is not a million miles away in character from Agatha Christie's parochial St Mary Mead and (paradoxically) this intimate focus might perhaps be why Läckberg is yet to make the breakthrough in the UK that is her due.

One would have thought that the perception that Läckberg has a certain congruence with the best-known female writer in crime fiction would hardly be a disincentive to readers. But current trends suggest that readers in the UK (and, to some extent, in the US) turn to Scandinavian crime fiction for its more edgy, abrasive characteristics – and the notion that Läckberg does not trade in this territory may have taken its toll. If that's the case, it is a great shame – although Läckberg echoes the cloistered setting of her English predecessor, the Swedish writer deals in far darker and more gruesome territory, with evil that has a wider reach. And despite the 'cosy' accoutrements, Camilla Läckberg is definitely not a writer (as they used to say in pre-politically correct days) for one's maiden aunt.

The Ice Princess Cometh

Proof that Läckberg is an uncompromising writer (despite the approachability of her work) is evinced by the first of her novels to be published in the UK, *The Ice Princess* (2002), although the book took several years to reach these shores. The parochial, Christie-style setting (sporting an assortment of characters with much to conceal) should be offset against the more stygian elements of the narrative – and a degree of understated, cold-eyed insight into modern Scandinavian society that places the writer firmly within the territory of her more abrasive colleagues. Writer Erica Falck returns to her hometown of Fjällbacka after the death of her parents, but finds that the sedate town has been turned upside down. One of Erica's childhood friends, Alex, has been murdered – and discovered in a grotesque situation. Her body has been discovered in a bath, her wrists cut open, her body encased in ice. She is, in fact, the eponymous Ice Princess. Erica decides to write about her very private friend, as much to reactivate her own stalled creative impulses as to find out what happened to the late Alex. Her investigation turns into something of an obsession, and when she begins to collaborate with local detective Patrick Hedström, the couple discover that underneath Fjällbacka's placid surface there is a wasps' nest of dangerous intrigue.

This impressive UK debut was followed by the equally unusual *The Stonecutter* (2005), also released in the UK some five years after its initial publication in Sweden, and the compelling *The Preacher* (2010). The latter was translated by the man who had originally rendered Stieg Larsson into English, the American Steven Murray; Murray and his translator wife Tina Nunnally have since taken turns to translate Läckberg's work. All of Läckberg's books (for all their apparent nods to the British golden age) are very much modern work, with an unsentimental view of human nature. *The Stonecutter,* for instance, begins with a grisly discovery: the corpse of a little girl found in a fisherman's net. Once again, it forces Patrick Hedström to track down a ruthless murderer, and the investigations by both Hedström and Erica Falck (their growing relationship is one of the pleasures of the series) encounter the customary wall of silence from the uncooperative townspeople. 2008's *The Drowning* is similarly provocative.

Unwanted Celebrity

The lively attention paid to Camilla Läckberg's private life (so unwelcome to the author) perhaps inevitably found its way into her work with *The Gallows Bird* (2006, published in the UK in 2011). The corrosive treatment of a brainless reality TV show (the UK's *Big Brother* is not alone in insulting the intelligence) perhaps suggests her own annoyance with the public focus on her relationship with the Swedish policeman who was the first winner of a reality show called *Survivor*. But the unsparing commentary on the idiocies of modern media is only one aspect of the book. In fact, all of Läckberg's work is (in subtle fashion) concerned with notions of identity. For the author, that identity is multifaceted; she is a modern woman, a highly successful writer, a celebrity, and a Swede. A coolheaded analysis of what it means to be all of these things can be found in her books, although never at the expense of persuasive narratives. And so too can such difficult issues as Sweden's occasional collusion with the Nazis, a theme that (like many of her colleagues) Läckberg addresses in her work, notably in the powerful

The Hidden Child (2007). The difficult situation of children born to Scandinavian mothers and German fathers is handled both responsibly and intelligently. Ironically, the very visible images of Läckberg herself in slightly kitsch angel wings to promote her novel *Angel Makers* (2011) might not do her any favours if she is genuinely concerned with downplaying the celebrity aspect of her life. (And the smiling image of a winged Läckberg as one of the women who actually murdered the children in their care may have one wondering just how thought-through the campaign was.) But her position as one of the most acclaimed of female Swedish crime writers is assured.

Upsetting the City Fathers: Liza Marklund

A trip down the sinister streets of Luleå in the company of **Liza Marklund's** investigative reporter Annika Bengtzon may not be in the tourist board brochure, but you won't quickly forget it. However, it wasn't in Luleå, but in a bright and breezy Copenhagen that I met Liza Marklund. Where to meet? An early morning coffee facing the famous Politiken's bookshop, a labyrinthine store with a distinctly quirky identity? We decide, in the end, to meet near a place now very familiar to obsessive viewers of the political thriller *Borgen* – the actual Borgen itself, the seat of government around which we see beleaguered Prime Minister Birgitte Nyborg preparing for her latest crisis as Secret Service men prowl nervously behind her. There were no signs of female prime ministers or guards as we strolled around the Tivoli Gardens (now shuttered and rather eerie) before settling down for a glass of wine at the Winter Garden in the Ny Carlsberg Glyptotek. I was to talk to Liza amid the massive fronds of the elegant cafe about death, dark deeds and journalism.

Maj Sjöwall apart, Marklund was the first important female Scandinavian crime novelist, with such books as the powerful *Red Wolf* or the tense new one, *Last Will*. Marklund, who radiates energy, was born in Piteå in northern Sweden, and has enjoyed something of a peripatetic lifestyle. 'I've lived in London, Jerusalem, America and Italy, among other places,' she tells me. 'My training was in journalism; now I also do... other things.' (These modestly omitted 'other things' include being a goodwill ambassador for UNICEF – she can be seen making a reasonable fist of singing an Abba song for a UNICEF TV programme.)

Her 1988 novel *The Bomber*, featuring resourceful reporter Annika Bengtzon, sold over half a million copies. It was, at that time, the most successful novel ever published in Sweden. 'A key perspective for my stories,' said Marklund, 'perhaps appropriate in Britain now as much as in Sweden, is media criticism and journalistic consequences – the power of the press, for good or ill. But I am absolutely a political writer. I use my novels to get a message across. I was always told that themes involving abused women and mistreated children didn't "sell". Nobody is more surprised – and gratified than me – that it isn't true...' But do we get an accurate picture of Scandinavian society, I ask, from its lacerating crime novels? 'For decades,' she replies, 'the Scandinavian media succeeded in spreading the picture of Scandinavia (and Sweden in particular) as Paradise on Earth. A lot of things are good here, but it's by no means heaven. We're way up there in the suicide league, for example. We drink too much, and too many men beat their women on a daily basis. Two of our major politicians have been murdered in the streets of Stockholm during the last 25 years, Olof Palme and Foreign Minister Anna Lindh (who was a very good friend of mine). So the pictures that British readers get through our crime novels are actually more correct than our propaganda brochures.'

The Godmother

She is far too young-looking for the soubriquet which has been accorded to her – but Lisa Marklund said to me that she doesn't mind being called 'The Godmother of Scandinavian Crime Fiction'. Of course, this accolade (however well-earned) rather complicates the female parentage of the whole genre: does that make the venerable Maj Sjöwall the grandmother? And where is Maria Lang in this parental hierarchy? But there is no question that the energetic Marklund is one of the most significant figures in the genre, with particular strands of her individual creativity that are unlike many of her colleagues – as we shall see. For those who take an interest in such things, the appearance of Lisa Marklund's name as co-author with the American writer James Patterson was something of a jaw-dropper. After all, surely Patterson only worked with writers we had barely heard of, however individually successful some of them may have proved later? But here was Patterson – a writer who seems to feel the need to produce more novels than the rest of us have read – teaming up with a truly significant foreign writer, one beginning to make the kind of breakthrough commensurate with her talent in the US and the UK that she deserved. (She already enjoys massive acclaim in her native Sweden as well as considerable German sales.) What was she up to, accepting this gig as a Patterson co-writer? Surely she should have it turned down? 'Not at all! Why should I have done?', she said to me. 'I enjoyed working on *The Postcard Killers* with James, and as the book had both American and Swedish central characters, our partnership was a logical one, wasn't it?' One might argue that however prodigious Patterson's sales, Marklund is the more accomplished writer, but I decided to let that pass. However, for those who know their Scandinavian crime fiction onions, it is the solus work of Lisa Marklund that commands the attention.

Marklund: The Facts

As mentioned earlier, Marklund was born in Piteå in northern Sweden but she prides herself on the gypsy in her soul. She has hung her hat in America and London (the source of her excellent English along with the excellent language teaching that is *de rigueur* in Swedish schools), as well as Italy and Jerusalem, her training in journalism leading to a series of prestigious newspaper jobs, perhaps most notably on *Expressen* and *Aftonbladet*. She has, she tells me, been a columnist and a journalist for 25 years, and has been particularly critical of the rosy picture of her society found in many of its newspapers. It's a picture she has been at some pains to correct with her often excoriating novels. Usually shot through with a keen feminism, her female protagonists are sometimes even more hostile to the male sex than Lisbeth Salander.

Marklund Alone

A good place to start with Marklund's impressive oeuvre is the trenchant *Red Wolf* (2003, ably translated by Neil Smith), and the two novels recently reissued in Britain, *The Bomber* (1998) and *Vanished* (2004), part of a sequence of novels featuring the tenacious *Evening Post* crime reporter Annika Bengtzon, something of a surrogate for the writer herself. *The Bomber* was a remarkable success, selling over half a million copies and bringing Marklund to a whole new audience, complementing the achievement of novels such as *Studio Sex* (1999). *The Bomber* is a clear example of just how much the work has progressed since her first book *On the Run* in 1995. That novel had a certain kinetic force, but this tense piece shows a writer much more in command of the tools of her trade. Two killings in Stockholm's international container port set things in motion, and a heady brew stirs in brutal Serbian criminals and a woman on the run from an implacable killer. And Annika Bengtzon, hired by a Swedish tabloid paper, is trying to cope with a killing she herself has committed: that of an abusive partner. What follows is a fast-moving narrative at the centre of which is the reporter's passion for justice – clearly a passion shared by her creator. The other major Marklund theme is the appalling treatment of women by the male sex (a recurrent motif of her work, making her sometimes read like Stieg Larsson *avant la lettre*), and, as with her late fellow Swede, the male reader may sometimes be made to feel that the whole sex is communally culpable for the way some brutal men behave towards women. *The Bomber* is something of a signature work, moving with an impressive velocity as it deals (intelligently) with its terrorist theme. (A watchable if workaday movie of the novel has been made under the title *Deadline*.) *Last Will* (2006, published in the UK in 2011) is also a key book.

Marklund said to me that she is happy to continue to deal with the specifics of her own country, but hopefully using it as a macrocosm for the rest of the world. She continues to call herself very much a political writer, and uses her novels to put across the points that she has expressed in her journalism over the last quarter of a century. Marklund smiles wryly at the fact that her books are now unquestionably commercial successes, when they were once described as unsaleable. Her topics (such as the maltreatment of women and children) were described as 'commercial poison' – and there is a grim satisfaction for her in the fact that such material is absolutely central to much current Scandinavian crime fiction.

'The abuse of power,' she says, 'is probably my central theme, whatever form it takes.' She is aware that she is one of the voices who have redressed the international balance in terms of an unrealistic picture of her country. 'People like myself are given to asking: if this is such a perfect country, why are our suicide figures so high? Having said that,' she continues, 'there is much that I love about my country, and I hope I express that along with any inherent criticism. Many of our problems – such as, for instance, the integration of immigrants into the host population – are common to other countries such as Britain. And as for Britain,' she smiles, 'I was relieved and pleased that *Red Wolf* appeared to be the book that really broke my name in the UK. But everybody seems to like that one – both here and abroad – would that were true of all one's work! The only people who seemed to object to the book were those from my hometown, who didn't like the characterisation of Piteå as cold and dark. But let's face it, *Red Wolf* is set in the Arctic Circle in the middle of winter – what other climactic conditions could I describe?'

I later asked Marklund (on a trip to the Harrogate crime festival) which of her books she was most proud of – and why. She pondered for a moment. 'Frankly, I can't really say that I'm particularly proud of any of my crime novels. That's not the reason I wrote them – to feel any pride – and it's not the emotion I associate with them. I wrote them because I wanted to (or maybe even because I had to). If I have any kind of feelings for them, it's joy and some sort of contentment. Maybe even a certain relief. But there's one book that I actually do feel a kind of pride about. It's a collection of articles, chronicles and essays that took me 25 years to write. I call it *New Voices Sing the Same Songs*. It contains my most controversial journalistic writing, the really difficult interviews, stories that show the development of law enforcement's ambitions to stop domestic violence and child abuse over the decades; cases I've followed for a quarter of a century. It covers politics and economics and international terrorism. But it also includes my most fatal mistakes, the really embarrassing moments, and the most personal (even private) stuff I've ever written (like the sensation of waking up in the wrong bed the morning after a very long night).'

As Marklund was clearly in frank mood, I decided to ask her about the work of her Scandinavian colleagues. Which book of their books would she most like to have written?

'I truly respect and admire the work of several of my colleagues,' she replies, 'but I can't honestly say that I would have liked to have written any of their books. The reason I started writing my own crime novels was that I felt there were none like them around at the time. I wanted to write about the topics that I couldn't get into the established mass media, the totally unsellable themes and issues that nobody cared about. The books I started to write were not supposed to sell. This was completely fine with me. I didn't go to any established publishing house (my first novel – not a crime one – was published by Bonniers, an experience I did not like and never wanted to be part of again). I wanted to write on my own terms, about my own topics, and have power over the entire publishing process – from printing to promotion. So I went to a friend who published his friends' books as a hobby. He promised to pay for the printing – but nothing else. This was totally fine, too. I never expected any money from my fiction writing. I had been producing stories for the biggest tabloid in Northern Europe for years, and had worked as the editor in chief of a morning daily and executive editor of Channel 4 News – I knew I could make a living as a freelance journalist, writing political reports on gender issues on the side. Consequently, the crime fiction was for fun and personal satisfaction.

Borrowing Annika

'One important part of my fiction writing was to be my protagonist. I wanted a heroine that I could identify with, a human being, and a woman – full of flaws and contradictions (smart and obnoxious, loving and unpleasant, clumsy and ambitious) – and with specifically female terms of reference and circumstances. I wanted her to have a job and kids and a husband and an unexciting sex life, a slight eating disorder and friends that used her for support and money. I wanted her to feel guilt when leaving her kids at daycare and guilt when leaving her job to go pick up the kids. I wanted her to cry too much and in the wrong places, to be an abused victim as well as – even – a killer, to love her children but dislike her mother. But – above all! – I was going to let her get away with it. She has a boss who supports her, colleagues who help her, she makes mistakes that few living women would survive and still be around, but she – somehow – makes it. In that sense, my Annika Bengtzon is also an incantation: if I keep writing about her long enough, maybe the rest of us will be allowed to be a little bit more like her.'

Marklund continues wryly: 'This actually works. I've had several colleagues coming up to me over the years, describing how they use Annika as a tool – when they are stuck in line somewhere, when people are pushing them around – they just get into character and start talking with the loud and unpleasant voice of Annika, demanding their rights. And she's up for grabs! Anybody who wants to can borrow her! With my pleasure!' Fellow novelist Tove Alsterdal told me that she considers *The Bomber* to be Marklund's most significant novel, probably because of its groundbreaking properties. 'She was the first to introduce a contemporary and complex female heroine into a landscape of ageing male detectives who spend their time listening to opera and lamenting the past. Liza took the Sjöwall & Wahlöö tradition of social political crime into the present day, and changed the crime genre in one swoop – a host of strong female characters followed in her footsteps, with Lisbeth Salander as perhaps the best-known example. I think that our strong female heroines – who actually behave like real women – are a key factor in the international success of the genre.'

Drowning in the Flowing Stream

The writer **Helen Tursten** has told me that she has a 'fear of drowning in the flowing stream of all the brilliant Scandinavian authors.' But she acknowledges that she has written books which she feels can hold their own with her rivals. But which books?

'I can't answer that,' she responds wryly. 'When I'm asked which book I am most proud of, the answer is: always the last one. An author always has to constantly try to become better. You have to write the text over and over again, until a voice says: "Yes, *now* it is working!" I would like to call it the "ticking feeling". It is like music: you can hear it clearly inside your head. If an author does not get that sensation, my advice is not to publish that novel. Rewrite it or just drop it in the bin. The book, though, that I would like most to have written is *Blackwater* (1993) by **Kerstin Ekman**. It is, I consider, a masterpiece. She presents everything the reader might want: beautiful natural settings, a horrible crime, fascinating characters, a breathtaking mystery and even a well-realised love story. She received the August Prize and the 1993 Best Crime Novel of the Year prize for the book, and, subsequently, the Nordic Council Literature Prize in 1994.'

Lofty Heights: Håkan Nesser

I was in Lund recently to meet a best-selling (and one of the best) Swedish crime writers, the drily witty – and unfeasibly tall – **Håkan Nesser**. Strolling around the well-preserved old town before a meeting for lunch, I was reminded of the fact that, Lund, with its imposing academic buildings and echoes of an English university town, is a good place to run into the bookish Nesser, as there are congruences with Oxford. After all, it was Colin Dexter, creator of the equally academic Morse, a man who could match Nesser's copper Van Veeteren for bookishness, who described the latter as being 'destined for a great place among the great European detectives.' The urbane, sometime-London-based novelist is very different from Larsson – or Mankell. 'What we have in common', he tells me, 'is that we all write (or wrote) in Swedish. Larsson had a different political perspective from me.' Håkan Nesser, in two separate series, has utilised separate locales. There is the not-quite-Sweden in his novels featuring his detective Van Veeteren, but the author's own country is the setting for those books in which the protagonist is Gunnar Barbarotti. Both series demonstrate why Nesser is held in such high esteem by both critics and readers; particularly notable is a more centrist political position than many of his more left-wing confrères.

Moral Choices

Key preoccupations of most of Nesser's work are the imponderables of moral choice, although such *crises de conscience* are usually resolved in decisive action rather than stasis. That is very much the case in *The Unlucky Lottery*, one of the writer's more unusual books, featuring a scenario in which four friends have their lives transformed when they win the lottery. But the tendentious title says it all: hours after the win, one of the group, Waldemar Leverkuhn, is discovered in his home, savagely stabbed to death. As we know from other books, Chief Inspector Van Veeteren is as interested in bibliographic matters as he is in the science of detection (perhaps more so) and is on sabbatical working in a second-hand bookshop. The case falls to his colleague Inspector Munster. Then another member of the lottery group vanishes, along with the neighbour of the murdered man, and it isn't long before the out-of-his-depth Munster is calling on his counterintuitive colleague for help. A visit to a psychiatric clinic opens up a new and disturbing aspect of the enquiry, and the secrets of the case begin to affect several lives. For many Nesser fans, this is a particular favourite among the writer's prodigious output, not least for its strange mixture of steady trajectory and halting, philosophical mien – a juggling act attempted by Nesser several times in his career.

'I was brought up in Kumla,' he tells me. 'It's the most prestigious prison town in Sweden, and it may have helped put me on the right criminal path (at least, the kind of criminal path where you're paid rather than arrested).' We talked about a recent novel of his to appear in the UK, *Hour of the Wolf*. 'The UK title isn't mine,' Nesser said. 'The original Swedish title referred to a game rather like billiards – not sinister enough, I suppose. I defer to the wisdom of my British publisher.' Does Nesser have a favoured child among his books? He sighs. 'I have no favourite, but that's a question I'm asked all the time. My wife Elke tells me I should have a stock answer: *The Shadows and the Rain* – the title is from a poem by Elizabeth Browning, by the way, which is quoted in the book – and over the years I have started realising Elke might have a point. Or I might perhaps pick my London novel from 2011 – *London Skies*. A great many Swedish and Danish readers tell me how much they like it. But when I think of the effort and the amount of thinking it took me to produce it, I still get a headache. None of the above are translated into English yet, so there will be no immediate objections to these choices, neither from you nor from your countrymen. Anyway, regarding my books, I think I have a strong case when I sincerely say: "Je ne regrette rien." Favourites by other writers? Peter Høeg's *Miss Smilla's Feeling for Snow*, of course... I would rewrite the last one hundred pages, but up till then it's a terrific book.'

Translation Talk

Laurie Thompson, the eminent (and entertainingly sardonic) translator of Henning Mankell and Håkan Nesser, is someone I always find to be a fund of often unsparing insights. 'As you know,' he told me, 'I'm not a crime specialist, and my involvement in Swedish (not Scandinavian) crime novels is accidental. I didn't watch *The Bridge* or *Borgen*; I did watch the last couple of Kenneth Branagh Wallander adaptations, and thought they were awful. My connection with Swedish crime novels lately has been via Håkan Nesser and Åsa Larsson. I have translated and submitted a Henning

Mankell novel, but it's not a crime novel; the Swedish title was *In Memory of a Dirty [or Mucky] Angel*, but I gather the publishers are going to call it *A Treacherous Paradise*. It's about a poverty-stricken girl from the north of Sweden who, thanks to a series of coincidences, ends up as the owner of the biggest and best-known brothel in southern Africa. Fascinating stuff, and a devastating attack on colonialism, but not a crime novel – although crimes are committed in it. Åsa Larsson's *Until Thy Wrath Be Past* was short-listed for the CWA Foreign Crime Dagger, but it was the Italians' turn. I've turned my attention to her book *The Sacrifice to Moloch*; the opening section I found very impressive and creepy: a bear kills and tries to eat a dog tethered to a leash in somebody's garden in the far north of Sweden, is shot and wounded but not killed, but then hunted down and the contents of its stomach suggest that it has been eating humans...

'I've also been working on a Håkan Nesser novel, called in Swedish *Ewa Moreno's Case*, but it will be called *The Weeping Girl* in English. It's a typical Nesser novel, full of linguistic jokes and amusing banter between police officers, quite horrific happenings, but it also raises questions about the human condition and human shortcomings. I think it's a brilliant piece. Similarly, his novel which in Swedish is called *The Swallow, the Cat, the Rose, Death*. Typical Nesser, raising questions about the human condition and comparing twisted human minds with those of cats. It's about a serial strangler and his psyche. The swallow and the cat in the title refer to an incident when a swallow flies through an open window into a bedroom, is captured by a cat, eventually killed and eaten but first tortured. Håkan wonders about the mentality of cats that apparently need to torture their prey before finishing them off and eating them: readers are invited to compare this with the mentality of the serial strangler. Also typical is that the rose reference is to William Blake's poem, 'The Sick Rose':

> O Rose thou art sick
> The invisible worm
> That flies in the night

In the howling storm
Has found out thy bed
Of crimson joy
And his dark secret love
Does thy life destroy.

It is quite a long way into the novel before we find out details of who the serial strangler actually is. Early on he strangles his wife while they are holidaying on a Greek island, and she tells him she loves somebody else. Then somebody picks up a woman in London and strangles her – it's not clear that it's the same man, but the reader is invited to put two and two together. Then a man who claims to be called Benjamin Kerran seduces first a manic depressive woman, and then her 16-year-old daughter, whose name is Monica Kummerle. He gives Monica a book of Blake's poetry, hence the rose reference. (It later transpires that his name is not Benjamin Kerran at all – that is a name 'stolen', I think, from a Victorian novel but you get the idea.) Both mother and daughter are duly strangled. Later on a couple of women friends check into an internet dating set-up and arrange to meet a man: he tries to strangle the one he meets, but she escapes. Typical of Håkan, apart from the learned references already mentioned, is the name of the 16-year-old girl. Her surname is Kummerle. "Kummer" is the German word for grief, sorrow, bother; and the ending "-le" is the southern German diminutive – so the implication is little (young) sorrowful one. Quite a lot of names in Håkan's novels have similar implications. A possible translation problem is whether/how to try to reproduce the implications in English. My general reaction is to leave them as they are and, like Håkan, leave it up to the reader to see the subtleties or not: if they do appreciate them, then their understanding of the novel is duly increased. If they don't, it doesn't really matter. These comments, I hope, help to illustrate why I think Håkan is a brilliant writer – one can appreciate and enjoy his novels without realising all the subtleties: but if you do, then he becomes even better!'

Dystopian Standalones

Another well-respected translator, the forthright **Sarah Death**, has similarly cogent views on Scandinavian writers. 'In 2011–12,' (she told me) 'I translated **Per Wahlöö's** *Murder on the Thirty-First Floor* and *The Steel Spring* for the British publisher Vintage. They were first published in 1964 and 1968 respectively, but the original English translations by the late Joan Tate have been out of print for many years. It has been said that Wahlöö's partner, Maj Sjöwall, was the one who injected the social and emotional perspective into their Martin Beck novels. It is certainly true that these two novels, dystopian standalones linked by their main protagonist, Inspector Jensen, are cleverly crafted but devoid of human warmth. Used as we have become to the husband-wife double act, this is a little like a duet with one voice missing. Jensen is a man who finds it very hard to relate to people in any way but the professional. The only character in the books given a name, he is a solitary, stoical, coolly calculating, crime-solving machine, fascinating to watch in action. His debilitating digestive problems could perhaps be seen as the prototype for the diabetes of Mankell's Wallander. The risky but vital organ transplant that Jensen undergoes abroad in *The Steel Spring* is a crucial plot device, but there is no chance of enjoying his restored health in the post-apocalyptic landscape that awaits him back home.

'The crimes in these novels are crimes against society perpetrated by vested interests; ordinary people are mere brainwashed pawns in the games of big business. When the vested interests are cynical media empires in league with coalition governments, it all feels very close to home for us in Britain today. The future painted in these novels is too like our own society for comfort: voter apathy is endemic, the media have relentlessly dumbed down their output, tasteless food and binge drinking are the norm and the car is king; pollution and refuse mountains will engulf us all unless pharmaceuticals kill us first; material well-being signally fails to bring happiness. Wahlöö's proposed solution is a radically left wing and egalitarian one. These books were relatively straightforward for the translator, but the question of period vocabulary had to be addressed. I could have made the language of the translation more retro, to match the original, but the editor preferred to go for a more neutral or timeless feel. It is always intriguing to see the past's vision of the future. In the lighter moments of the translation task I felt as if I were in an episode of *Thunderbirds*, in a world of multilane highways, flyovers and plastic furniture, where men still wear hats and computers have somehow failed to get invented.'

I spoke to Sarah Death about another book she'd worked on – a very different kettle of fish.

'I recently translated another police procedural, but of completely different style and vintage: **Kristina Ohlsson's** *Silenced* (a follow-up to *Unwanted*). A police procedural inevitably involves not just the officers but also the translator in a lot of fairly mundane and repetitive work, but *Silenced* really takes wing when it moves out into the world, particularly in the sequences describing the nightmare that engulfs a young woman stranded far from Sweden. Kristina Ohlsson, now with four bestselling crime novels to her name in Sweden, has given up her job as a counter-terrorism researcher to write full-time. It will be interesting to see how her work is reflected in the plots and characters of her coming books.'

Black Paths: Åsa Larsson

Lashings of atmosphere distinguish **Åsa Larsson's** uncompromising fiction, with Sweden's northernmost town, Kiruna, her protagonist Rebecka Martinsson's bolthole. There is a splendid piece of sleight-of-hand at the beginning of one of the most accomplished novels by the Swedish Crime Queen. And it is a tactic which both wrongfoots the reader and (simultaneously) imparts some vivid local colour, reminding us that we are reading a novel set an ocean away from London or Manchester. A man is sitting fishing on a spring evening in Torneträsk. At this time of year, the residents make the trip to a secluded area where the ice is more than a metre thick, riding snowmobiles, and towing their 'arks' behind them. These arks, we learn, are small fishing cabins with a hole in the floor. Using this hole, the fishermen drill through the ice, and sit inside fishing warmed by a Calor gas stove. But the fisherman we meet in *The Black Path* is unlucky. Stepping outside in his underwear to relieve himself, he watches in horror as his ark is whipped away by a storm. He knows that when he finds it, it will be matchwood, and that his chances of survival are slim – unless he finds another ark. Which he does, stumbling across a deserted one. He breaks in, wrapping himself in the two pairs of long johns he finds inside. He sees a blanket on the camp bed and pulls it off. And underneath it lies the body of a woman, her eyes frozen into an icy stare. It is at this precise point that the reader realises that this stunningly described early chapter is, in fact, a clever revision of one of the oldest clichés in the crime thriller lexicon: the discovery of the corpse that sets the plot in motion.

But those who have read her earlier book *The Savage Altar* will know that Asa Larsson would not be content to travel well-worn paths; every element of her work, however familiar it may be, is always granted an idiosyncratic new twist. And while many Nordic crime writers are often content to locate their bloody deeds in suburban cities not unlike those of Britain, Larsson is always looking for the more off-kilter setting. And the Sweden we see in her books is not that to be found in other writers – certainly not the locale that her late male namesake utilised. Present and correct in this latest book is her distinctive female protagonist: the attorney Rebecka Martinsson, desperate to return to work after a grisly case that shredded her sanity, and the lone wolf policewoman Anna-Maria Mella, who is handed the gruesome murder that begins the book. The woman's body has extensive evidence of torture, and there is a puzzling detail: underneath her workout clothes, she is wearing seductive lingerie. What's more, the victim is a key employee in a mining company with a global reach. Martinsson and Mella – as in previous outings – find their work cut out in the face of corruption and lethal perversion. Åsa Larsson aficionados will know that her duo of distaff investigators are among the most quirkily and individually characterised in the field (no easy task in a genre awash with damaged female protagonists), but the author's grasp of all her characters' psychology always possesses a keen veracity. And there is one more thing to praise here: Larsson's surefooted use of language, more elegantly structured than most of her crime writing rivals, notably so in Marlaine Delargy's characteristically flavoursome translation.

Speaking to Larsson when I moderated a panel with her at Bristol's CrimeFest, I asked her about her work, and received a frank reply. 'I'm most proud of my first novel, *The Savage Altar/Sun Storm*,' she said. 'I felt brave when I wrote it! I turned down a high-profile job as a tax lawyer because I knew that if I took it, it would mean working late nights and weekends, and the novel would probably never be written. Instead, I took a position as an administrative official at a court – which my lawyer friends thought was like me working at the checkout at a local supermarket. They said: "Åsa, the train is leaving, and you're still on the platform". They didn't know that I was working on a novel, and, frankly, I was too afraid to tell them. I also dared to write about things that were very shameful to me at the time: my own sense of inferiority in relation to my lawyer friends from the south of Sweden, with daunting upper-middle-class and upper-class backgrounds. I also had Rebecka hail from the small northern mining town of Kiruna, where people don't really know "how to behave"… at least not in the eyes of the Southerners. And I'm proud that I finished it. I had young children. A husband. A job. A house and a large garden and friends – everyone wanted a piece of me. But I built an iron fence around myself and the novel, and said: "This is my time." Looking back on it, I wonder if there will ever be a bigger moment for me than when I finished the last sentence of that book. Who inspires me personally? Well, I wish I had written *Blackwater* by **Kerstin Ekman**. She is one of Sweden's most prominent novelists and when she chooses to write a crime novel she really raises the bar for the genre.'

The Cruel Stars of the Night: Kjell Eriksson

During the torrentially rainy summer of 2012, the British book trade may have suffered from a lack of footfall, but one trend continued to steam ahead relentlessly: the continuing invasion of Scandinavian crime writers. Those with vision welcomed the appearance of a variety of books by the gifted **Kjell Eriksson**, winner of the Swedish Crime Academy Award for Best Crime Novel and a distinctive and unusual talent. It was also interesting to note that for the promotion of his work, Eriksson's publisher utilised something of a new approach: actually mentioning on the jacket that his translator was Ebba Segerberg, responsible for the idiomatic translation of John Ajvide Lindqvist's *Let the Right One In*. Certainly, for translators used to smarting from disregard, this was a welcome trend. *The Cruel Stars of the Night* (2004), featuring Eriksson's signature character Inspector Ann Lindell, will serve as an auspicious introduction to readers new to this Swedish writer. Winter is laying its frigid hand on the Swedish city of Uppsala, when an elderly professor, Ulrik Hindersten, vanishes without a trace. The disappearance is reported by his daughter, Laura whose disturbed inner life is described by the author to (initially) puzzling – but significant – effect. Shortly after, two local farmers are discovered within days of each other, beaten to death, and it is up to Inspector Ann Lindell to discover a connection between the crimes. But on this occasion, the solution to the mysteries may not be under her nose but in distant parts. There is a direct and unadorned quality to Eriksson's prose (as rendered in Segerberg's highly professional translation) which is actually somewhat deceptive. Beneath the straightforwardly rendered narrative, there is a pronounced poetic sensibility here – unforced and unobtrusive, certainly, but granting *The Cruel Stars of the Night* a more elusive quality than most Nordic crime fiction. The unsparing elements of the narrative are productively played out against a vein of black humour. I asked Eriksson (who suggested to me that there are a dozen bad Swedish writers for every Henning Mankell) which books of his had pleased him most. 'It's hard to choose one of my books in the Lindell series as the most satisfying,' he replied. 'Perhaps *The Princess of Burundi*, for a sentimental reason: it is set in the neighbourhood where I was born and raised, which is the working-class area of Uppsala, some distance from the famous University. Actually, thinking about it, all my books – in one way or another – deal with the contradictions created by the fact there are two Uppsalas. It's a divided city.'

Demons

Readers curious as to why Henning Mankell should provide Eriksson with a generous encomium ('Eriksson's crime novels are among the very best') need look no further than 2005's *The Demon of Dakar*, which along with such highly individual offerings as *The Hand that Trembles* and *The Princess of Burundi* are further proof that this is a writer who (while resembling in most respects his fellow Nordic crime writers) is actually subtly different. Once again we are in the company of his tenacious policewoman Ann Lindell, and we are also in the vividly realised Uppsala which Eriksson has previously conjured with such panache. A naked man is found in a river, his neck mutilated and the only clue to his identity is what remains of a tattoo, partially scraped off his arm. Lindell becomes involved when a drug deal goes badly wrong, and a man is hospitalised with a mutilation similar to the one found on the man in the river. Lindell begins to see a connection with the local Dakar restaurant, whose proprietor is the sybaritic Slobodan Andersson. There is a heady mix of elements stirred into the brew with *The Demon of Dakar*, including blackmail, drug running and kidnapping, all handled with the rigour we have come to expect from Eriksson. But perhaps the most rewarding element here is the commanding characterisation, such as that of the gluttonous restaurateur, a character worthy of such masters as Eric Ambler.

It Can't Happen Here: Tomb of Silence

At Krimimessen: the leading Scandinavian crime fiction festival (held at a decommissioned prison in Horsens, Denmark), I spoke to another highly-thought-of Swedish writer, **Tove Alsterdal**, and asked her which of her books she was most proud of. 'If I have to choose,' she replied, 'it would have to be the latest, *Tomb of*

Silence, which appeared in Sweden in 2012 – it has yet to be published in the UK. I was keen to write about Tornedalen – the Swedish borderland to the east, way up north, where my family is from. It's Sweden, but a totally different Sweden from the popular image, far away from the small idyllic towns that have become something of a cliché in Swedish crime. You know, those places where people live in innocent harmony, away from the rest of the world, until a murder is committed and everyone shouts in dismay: "HOW could this happen HERE?" For me, that's a Sweden that – frankly – I don't recognise at all, and I'm actually not sure it even exists – or has ever existed. It's like dream land from childhood.

'In Tornedalen, on the other hand, people are aware that violence and evil always exist somewhere. It's a region of strong conflicts, no doubt because of its proximity to the East. When my oldest aunt was born, it was the Tsars' Russia on the other bank of Torne River, just a few hundred metres away. During the First World War this was the only gate between Western and Eastern Europe, and my mother grew up watching the neighbouring farms burn in acts of Nazi vengeance.

'In the 1930s, in some of the villages here, one third of the population were Nazis, one third hard-headed communists, and the rest were devotees of a local religious movement, waiting for the holy Silver Ark to land on Torne River and take them to the Heavenly Jerusalem. *Tomb of Silence* takes place in the present day, but stretches back to this era, as well as into the East, to the almost mythical Karelia and the former Soviet Union, as well as today's Russia. It's certainly a work of crime fiction, but simultaneously a historical novel and a dark family tale. I wanted to freight in the crime elements, and let them unfold and grow. My philosophy? Give the reader more than they expected, but without losing the tension and driving force of the crime novel. To me crime fiction isn't just entertainment; I write in the social political tradition, but I also want to strain the boundaries of the genre, to see how far I can take it.'

The taxi that took me to the celebrated Krimimessen festival wound up a hill towards the louring prison which can be seen from almost everywhere in the town. This is a prison city, much like the prison town Håkan Nesser grew up in. But the prison itself is long decommissioned, with well-fed festival attendees sipping wine in its exercise yards, and is now an appropriate venue for a crime festival with serious literary gravitas. The prison, as I strolled its grounds, was full of authors, principally Scandinavian but with a sprinkling of Brits including myself, Andrew Taylor, SJ Bolton and SJ Watson. It was pleasant to say hello to all these writers, of course, but I was there for the Scandinavians, and over the next couple of days I had a chance to make contact with several stellar talents – some whom I'd met before and some who were new to me.

Echoes: Johan Theorin

An old friend is **Johan Theorin** (usually seen – as I see him in Denmark – in trademark black cap), whose resonant *Echoes from the Dead* (2007) is easily one of the most distinctive novels in the invasion of Nordic crime writers. Its prize-winning status in both Sweden and Britain is massively justified, as is that of his equally distinguished book, *The Quarry*. Theorin takes the reader on unsettling trips to the Swedish island of Öland, and the ambience of a blowy off-season Swedish island is handled with consummate skill.

If the truth be told, there are several writers in the current all-conquering Scandinavian wave who write in similar fashion to each other – and there's nothing wrong with that. The tough police procedural, with its vision of the cracks in the social fabric, has plenty of mileage yet – as key practitioners from Henning Mankell onwards continue to prove. But if you've acquired a taste for something more subtle and allusive, there is one writer who deserves to be on your reading list: Mr Theorin. Unlike those of most of his confrères, Theorin's books are poetic, atmospheric pieces with a precise attention to the dark psychological state of the characters. His novels are leavened with a certain fey non-naturalistic quality, and the island of Öland to which he repeatedly draws us is as unsettling and mysterious a location as we will find anywhere in modern Nordic noir. However, if we come to a recent book, *The Asylum*, with these expectations in place, we are in for a rude shock. When I mentioned to Theorin that I was looking forward to reading this book (originally called *Saint Psycho's* – a much more apposite title), Theorin was at some pains to point out that this was very different from his customary work – and it most assuredly is that. All of the qualities which distinguished such books as *The Darkest Room* and *Echoes of the Dead* are satisfyingly in place, but the new book is more direct and visceral than his earlier work. The name of the asylum in the book, he mentioned, has a personal significance. Swedish hospitals are usually named after patron saints, and the 'Patricia' in the name of the asylum 'Saint Patricia's' is a guiding light of Theorin's own: the American writer Patricia Highsmith.

Visiting Saint Psycho's

The Asylum takes the reader into the troubled life of preschool teacher Jan Hauger, who has a new job at an isolated nursery – but this is no ordinary pre-school kindergarten. There are subterranean passages leading from the nursery to an adjoining asylum, Saint Patricia's – known locally as Saint Psycho's after its highly dangerous inmates, including some of the country's most murderous psychopaths. Part of the therapy for the inmates is to allow carefully supervised visits by their children living in the nursery – visits that can be made via the gloomy tunnels. As this gothic premise suggests, we are into darker territory than even Theorin has tackled previously, and if the reader is tempted to assign Freudian interpretations to the dark passageways here, they will not be far off the mark. But although the novel has a more straightforward engagement with the mechanics of generating suspense than we're used to from Theorin, we have learnt that he is a writer who enjoys pulling the metaphorical rug from beneath our feet – and that is a tactic that he employs several times here. Apart from anything else, the callow hero Jan is (we slowly learn) not all that he appears to be. A damaging incident from his teenage years has traumatised him and even led to a suicide attempt, and he has an unhealthy obsession with a girl named Alice Rami – an obsession he has been unable to shake. But most worrying of all is Jan's kidnapping of a child. There are few more disturbing passages in modern crime fiction than that in which we see Jan begin to prepare a subterranean cell for the child he is planning to kidnap, and it is all the more queasy for the reader because we have become so thoroughly placed in Jan's consciousness. There may be those who do not welcome this striking change of pace from the more nuanced territory of his customary work, but in fact *The Asylum* is every bit as authoritative a piece of writing as anything that Johan Theorin has given us. What's more, after this book, who knows into what new and nightmarish directions he will strike out ? All bets, it seems, are off...

Into the Darkness

I ask Theorin if *The Darkest Room* is the book in which he feels he came closest to what he was attempting to do as a writer. 'Perhaps,' he replies carefully. 'Actually, I've noticed that readers always want to tell me about their own favourites of the novels I have written. Usually, à propos of your question, it is *The Darkest Room*, but the other books also have their fans. Favourite book, though... But you'll have to forgive a classic author answer: To me, my novels are like my children, and I like them all. Oh – and I suppose I should note that I have some objections to them all, as well. But, inevitably, the debut novel is of course always special, especially since it also was my breakthrough here in Sweden. So my answer is: *Echoes from the Dead*. I tried to write a very personal crime novel about a place (the island of Öland) which means a lot to me, with a fictitious story, but hopefully informed by honest emotions I have experienced myself.

'I don't really have a secret wish that I'd written any other novels than my own. I am not a very envious person. Usually I just envy other authors' knowledge of things that I know very little about, such as medicine (doctors who write crime fiction impress me) or weapons (I hate weapons, but would like to be an authority on them, even so) or... just about anything else. I wish I was an expert on something. I'm a jack of all trades... I just know a little about a lot of things ... But there are, of course, many Scandinavian crime novels which I have enjoyed and admire, and my three favourites are probably *The Laughing Policeman* by Sjöwall & Wahlöö, *Calling Out For You/The Indian Bride* by Karin Fossum and *Hour of the Wolf/Carambole* by Håkan Nesser. They are all rather different from each other, but distinctive in their own ways. I have also a few older favourites from my reading youth, such as *Gammal ost* by Ulf Durling, *Någon slog tillbaka* by K Arne Blom, *Berättelse för herr Hugo* by Jean Bolinder and *Kung Liljekonvalje av Dungen* by Maria Lang – but most of these are not translated and perhaps nowadays not very well known, even in Sweden.'

The Lacerating Mr Lapidus

Packing my bag for Sweden in 2012, and a trip to Ystad, a town very familiar to viewers of multiple TV series, filled me with pleasurable anticipation. But before that, two other Swedish cities were on my itinerary – at one of them I was to meet an author for inclusion in this book. Firstly, I'm crossing the mist-shrouded Oresund Bridge, famous now to devotees of the BBC Series *The Bridge* (with not a single dismembered body to be seen), on my way to the architecturally striking Malmö, capital of Skania County. It may be beautiful, but this is the Nordic city with the most crime and the highest murder rate.

Malmö has one landmark which is an extremely appropriate image for a trip such as mine with its criminal agenda: a striking sculpture of a twisted gun. (It is, in fact, a monument to a victim of murder, John Lennon.) It is not a city, however, where the fingerprints of the criminal classes are evident to a tourist such as myself – but they'll certainly be well known to a lawyer-cum-writer such as **Jens Lapidus.** I last met him in the UK, and I've never encountered the writer when he has not looked well groomed and sharply dressed. It's a proper pride in his appearance that clearly appeals both to his legal clients and publishing people, and any discussion with him shows his equal enthusiasm for both worlds – which are perhaps less dissimilar than most of us would think. 'When you last saw me', Lapidus smiles, 'I was juggling my legal and writing careers.' (He's referring to an ever-jingling mobile phone during our last meeting – an insistent client.) 'But I'm on a writing tour now. I'll be talking about *Easy Money*.' This book offers a lacerating view of crime and Swedish society couched in vivid, idiomatic language evoking the American James Ellroy (who is a Lapidus fan). A massive success in Sweden, it has been adapted into a film. 'Actually, I'm fairly happy with the movie,' he tells me, 'mainly because they got the casting right. My characters, I hope, are unlike those of other Nordic writers – I didn't want them looking like standard criminals in the film. I know I'm part of the Scandinavian wave, but I really try to do something more international in flavour.'

Deceptions: Karin Alvtegen

The sometimes fractious relationship between the sexes is often at the heart of the complex and interesting writing of **Karin Alvtegen**. Her characterful 2003 novel *Missing* bagged the Nordic prize for Best Crime Novel (previous recipients have included Henning Mankell), and it begins in provocative and arresting fashion with a young woman in the sumptuous surroundings of the grand hotel in Stockholm, exquisitely accoutred and making a play for a middle-aged businessman. But she is not, as the reader might initially think, a prostitute – however, although there is no sexual consummation, the businessman finds that there is a price to play for his dalliance. In fact, the young woman, Sibylla, is one of the city's homeless, masquerading (in a kind of secret identity) as the sort of sybaritic, well-dressed creature she might like to be. The police are on her tail, however, and she discovers that the businessman has been found dead – and she, inevitably, is the principal suspect. While this not-so-hapless young woman is kept at the centre of a crisp, fast-moving narrative, Alvtegen shores up her novel with a rich seam of social commentary on her country, ensuring that the psychological underpinnings of her characters are set against a series of strikingly delineated social settings. Subsequent books by Alvtegen have shown a pronounced concern for the exploitation and abuse of vulnerable children (a theme she shares with the writer Liza Marklund) and some of her work features no crime elements at all. A recurrent preoccupation of her books is the immense difficulty people find in trying to change either their circumstances or their essential character – difficult, but not impossible, Alvtegen maintains.

The Mysterious Mr Dahl

Arne Dahl's *The Blinded Man* (2010) is the first novel in his accomplished 'Intercrime' sequence (already highly successful in Germany and the Nordic countries), and published in the UK by Vintage. Dahl is quiet and serious; he's looking forward, he tells me (not entirely convincingly) to his trip to Britain when his new publishers plan to re-launch him in the UK. In several ways, 2012 was a significant year for Scandinavian crime fiction on foreign shores – not least for the relaunch of certain Nordic writers in translation whose nimble work had previously either passed unnoticed or (sadly) withered on the vine. One of these was Åsa Larsson; the other was her fellow Swede, the quietly spoken and intense Arne Dahl. Despite his relative youth, Dahl belongs to that cadre of writers influenced by the unvarnished writing of Sjöwall & Wahlöö, with those writers' police department ethic transmuted into the younger writer's very different style. Dahl, who appears to possess the customary Scandinavian talent of bagging a slew of literary awards, is, in fact, a literary critic himself. His obvious love of language (not always a default virtue where crime writers are concerned) finds keen expression in his work – particularly so in the adroit Tiina Nunnally translation of the first book in Dahl's much-acclaimed Intercrime series, *The Blinded Man*. (British writers had previously had an opportunity to acquaint themselves with Dahl's book under the title *Misterioso*.) This is crime writing of genuine authority, and its sinewy, uncompromising structure marks Dahl out from many of his more discursive colleagues. Two influential Swedes, members of the country's elite, have been killed, and the crime has generated something of a mini-hysteria. It becomes politically pressing to inaugurate a task force to track down the murderer, and Detective Paul Hjelm is dragooned into the team. This comes as something of a surprise to him, given that he is in bad odour with the force and under investigation for misconduct because he has shot a man who took a bank hostage. So the new assignment offers Hjelm a chance for recapturing the kudos attached to his name – until he and the team realise just what an uphill struggle they have. Their highly intelligent nemesis has stripped the scene of crime of all possible clues, even removing the bullets. And it is only a matter of time before he kills again.

Sharing a Secret

For those non-Scandinavians who had already realised just how good Dahl was, there is a certain wistfulness in the realisation that his fame is about to spread – after all, it's always good to be an insider, party to knowledge not in the current domain. But Dahlians will simply have to grit their teeth and share their enthusiasm – not least as the second novel in the sequence, *Bad Blood*, is also launched in the UK. Dahl's impressive *Chinese Whispers* was nominated for the Glass Key award, having already bagged the Swedish Academy of Crime Writers Award for Best Crime Novel of the Year. His celebrity in Sweden is assured, not least by the cult success enjoyed by the ten-episode TV adaptation of *Misterioso* (the original title of *The Blinded Man*). It was calculated that over 15 per cent of the country's population watched the series in 2011. It is, however, the book that counts, and Dahl's command of his literary medium is never in doubt. In a fairly audacious strategy, he resists the temptation to generate suspense artificially, and allows the narrative to play out at a challenging, measured pace – and it is a strategy that pays dividends. Like so much Nordic fiction, the novel's concerns remain topical – not least for the financial doldrums the country is plunged into here. In Dahl's narrative, this is because of the ruthless elimination of rich individuals, rather than the mendacious behaviour of bankers. The devastating financial effect, however, is the same, with the banks on the point of imploding. And the newly created task force has its job complicated by other growing fears over potential terrorist atrocities, and ever-more-pressing problems with immigrants.

The book's appearance in the UK in 2012 may suggest that Dahl was inspired by the banking crisis of later years, but it should be remembered that *The Blinded Man* was published a decade before, demonstrating that (once again) crime writers can be more prescient than other scribes. The book was published second in the *Intercrime* series in Sweden, but was, in fact, the first in the sequence. It affords particular pleasure with its ill-matched team of police officers who are (as mentioned earlier) out of Sjöwall & Wahlöö via Ed McBain's squabbling 87th precinct cops (the inspiration for Martin Beck and co.). For those readers prepared to adapt to the initially steady pace (and who can keep track of his large dramatis personae), Dahl is undoubtedly a practitioner of the Nordic noir genre worth investigating. I spoke to his British publisher, Alison Hennessey, discussing the ten-book Intercrime series, a fixture on European bestseller lists since the publication of the first book in the late 1990s. 'What makes Dahl such a strong writer,' she said, 'is his desire to bring the high values of what we could traditionally term "literary fiction" to the crime genre; his characters are nuanced and his plotting assured. Across the series, Dahl explores the emotional development of a conventional police detective whilst tackling a range of moral issues. He also appears to possess an uncanny prescience; the first two books were written over twelve years ago yet their subjects, anger against banks and their irresponsible lending and US/Middle Eastern tensions over oil, are as topical as ever.'

A Cadre of Swedish Scribes

The talented **Alexander Söderberg** has achieved an overdue moment in the UK sun with the British publication of his thriller *The*

Andalucian Friend in 2013. The book is the first in a trilogy, and as an indication of the literary company he keeps, the author is from the same stable as Jo Nesbo and Arne Dahl, the prestigious Salomonsson Agency. Söderberg is also an in-demand scriptwriter, and he has adapted Camilla Läckberg's and Åke Edwardson's novels for Swedish TV. (Läckberg has expressed her approval of the adaptation.) Söderberg is the real deal – and *The Andalucian Friend* is one of the most significant entries in the Swedish wave. At a concert hall restaurant on London's South Bank, overlooking a darkening Thames, the author, quiet and personable, talked to me about the horses he raises in Sweden – and about his trilogy of novels which begins with the stunning and ambitious book. 'My protagonist,' he began, 'is a nurse called Sophie Brinkman – or to be more precise, she's one of my protagonists. I wanted her to be relatively ordinary; she's a nurse, a widow and a single mother. But Sophie finds herself drawn to the ambiguous figure of Hector Guzman, who is not only a publisher but the head honcho of an Andalucian crime ring specialising in transatlantic drug transactions. By becoming involved with him, Sophie finds herself in the middle of the clash of two international criminal groups – not to mention corrupt officers of the Swedish police force. I wanted the stakes to be high and I wanted a large canvas of characters – I found that a really stimulating challenge.' Had the writer's working in Swedish television, adapting Camilla Läckberg books such as *The Stone Cutter*, for the screen been useful training for him when he wrote his own novel sequence? 'Not really,' he replied. 'The secret of success, I learned, when it comes to television adaptation is precisely what to leave out – not quite the case when you're writing a fairly ambitious, large-scale novel sequence. The two disciplines are so different, and I don't really think they have very much in common.'

Söderberg's UK publisher, Liz Foley (who also numbers Jo Nesbo among her authors), spoke to me about him with justified pride. 'At Harvill Secker, we've been publishing crime fiction for a long time – and it's been really interesting in the last year or so to see the genre broadening out and extending from what some might see as its original conventions. Alexander Söderberg's *The Andalucian Friend* may be Swedish, but it is very much an international thriller, brimming with fast-paced action sequences taking place in a variety of countries – and not a lonely cabin in the snow in sight! Whereas **Antti Tuomainen's** *The Healer* (another of our books) does use the character of Helsinki more characteristically, as a key element of the narrative. But this is skewed by the fact that the novel takes place in a post-apocalyptic near-future. It's a very exciting time to be publishing work from the Nordic countries as the quality of the writing we're seeing is so high and the new creative directions authors are taking are really challenging.'

Camilla Ceder is a much respected writer, whose *Babylon* is a characteristically well-crafted book. The novel has Inspector Christian Tell and his team called to the scene of a double murder. University lecturer Anne-Marie Karpov lies dead in her home, alongside her student and lover, Henrik. The crime appears straightforward: Henrik's girlfriend Rebecca, a woman in therapy for her violent jealousy, had been spotted outside Karpov's flat, and her fingerprints are found on the door. But shortly afterwards, when Rebecca's flat is burgled in a seemingly unconnected attack, Tell begins to wonder whether she might be the victim in a larger game. It emerges that items on the Red List of artefacts raided from Iraqi museums were found among Henrik's possessions.

The eminent translator Marlaine Delargy (one of the most highly regarded in the field) told me she found this book much more assured than Ceder's first novel, *Frozen Moment*. The story of the relationship between the books' central characters, Christian Tell and Seja Lundberg, is developed with real skill, she noted, and forms an interesting counterpoint to the jealousy that lies behind the murders he is investigating (Seja is Tell's girlfriend; they met when he was investigating the murders in *Frozen Moment*, and she used her skills as a trainee reporter to carry out an investigation of her own, which very nearly scuppered the relationship).

Gothenburg in western Sweden hosts Scandinavia's biggest book fair, and the chilly countryside around the city is where Ceder explores the darkest recesses of the human psyche. Ceder (who herself lives in Gothenburg) originally studied social science and psychotherapy, disciplines that she has put to trenchant and intelligent use in her new vocation of psychological crime fiction – though she has not given up the day job, and continues to work in counselling and social work. That debut novel, *Frozen Moment* (2010), also has an adroit evocation of the cold countryside around Gothenburg, though she is particularly exercised by the darker psychological impulses of her characters (hardly surprising, given the other disciplines within which she works). *Babylon* continues her upwards trajectory.

Is the area of Östergötland as fey and otherworldly as **Mons Kallentoft** renders it? And is it as dangerous? Books such as the idiosyncratic *Summertime Death* (2008) offer a tentative answer. The book enjoyed a healthy stint on the Swedish bestseller lists, while other things added lustre to his celebrity: a three-book deal with a Swedish publisher, and a film deal that included *Midwinter Sacrifice*, *Summertime Death* and two other novels. Kallentoft's work is distinctly unorthodox in approach, and his achievement is of a different order from most of his colleagues – but his vision is one of the strangest and most allusive in the whole field.

Then there is the formidable **Leif Persson**. In his native Sweden, Persson the man is markedly more famous than his books; a situation looking set to change. He is a formidable criminologist who has appeared (with calculated comments) on Sweden's equivalent to the British TV show *Crimewatch*. A characteristic novel is the weighty *Another Time, Another Life*. A much talked-up writer who appeared in the UK in 2012 is **Jan Wallentin**, whose *Strindberg's Star* is a book that detonated on to the European literary scene in 2011, selling hundreds of thousands of copies in Scandinavia and Germany.

A Blast of Winter

Åke Edwardson, who first made his mark as a journalist, has created highly distinctive characters in his Inspector Erik Winter and the latter's senior, more saturnine colleague Ringmar. The city locales of Edwardson's novels are crammed full of persuasive detail about day-to-day life in modern Scandinavian cities, with the police routines echoing the 87th Precinct novels of Ed McBain. In the memorable *Winter*, we have the classic ill-at-ease copper continually under the cosh and suffering from a series of existential crises. *Frozen Tracks* (2001), set in Gothenburg, was serviceable, but the author's *Sun and Shadow* (2005), the first of his novels to be published in Britain, had a mesmerising grip in its tale of policemen Morelius and Bartram dealing with (among other things) the residues of untrammelled teenage drinking. Jazz aficionado (and sharply dressed) Erik Winter is facing the fateful four-zero, and is 'no longer the youngest chief inspector in Sweden'; he is soon tackling several murders that test his skills to the limit. But how satisfying – really – to a novelist is a *succès d'estime*? Is it enough to be thought of in the most glowing terms by a select band of aficionados when less talented writers are selling shedloads of books much inferior to your own? In fact, Edwardson is something more than a connoisseur's choice (although the Swedish novelist is certainly that) but for a writer of such accomplishment, his sales (in the UK at least) are not commensurate with his level of achievement – a situation that will, hopefully, change. The locale of Sweden's second-largest city, Gothenburg, is crucial to his books, as is the character of the fortyish copper at the centre of the narratives (who nourishes a love of jazz – a characteristic almost as *de rigueur* as a taste for drink). *Sun and Shadow* has a lengthy (and impressively organised) timeframe with an all-inclusive picture of a police station. The pithy dialogue is well realised in Laurie Thompson's typically idiosyncratic translation. The tenth appearance of Åke Edwardson's police inspector, *The Final Winter* (2008), provided something of a moratorium, with the author now seemingly impatient with the straitjacket of the detective novel form – but with all the energy and inventiveness of the earlier books present.

Emotional Scars

Personal experience is at the heart of a bestselling novel from another skilled Swedish crime writer: **Carin Gerhardsen's** compelling *The Gingerbread House*. Much of the traumatic childhood bullying in the novel is based on the author's personal experiences from her youth. Gerhardsen swapped her career as a mathematician for an IT career. But it was as a writer – with a celebrated crime trilogy – that she made her mark. These three books – the *Hammarby* series – were succeeded by other, equally distinctive work, such as *Gideon's Ring* (2012). Speaking to Gerhardsen about the book, I found her still exercised by childhood emotional scars. '*The Gingerbread House* is a novel about evil – and the consequences of a horrible childhood,' she told me. 'It's also concerned with issues of how disrespect from the people around you will ruin your self-confidence, and compromises your hopes for the future. As a child, I was subjected to intimidation and harassment myself, so the plot of the book came easily to me. Many of the scenes in the novel are versions of my own experiences. I wanted to explore how different people react to traumatic experience, and how bad childhood experiences can distort our adult lives. It's a crucial tenet for me that we all should take responsibility for the well-being of the people around us. And – now that I consider it – that particular aspect of life is always somehow involved in my stories: people who care and people who don't, people who react intelligently to what life throws at us and those who don't. How we all have a way of confronting complicated situations – and how some of us are shattered by our experiences.

'My work is always, frankly, rather sad,' she continued, smiling. 'I know that I personally enjoy suffering while reading! It's everyone's duty to be informed about what's going on in the world around us. That's why most of us watch the news and sometimes even take action concerning what we see. It's all about empathy, which is a gift vouchsafed to the human race, even though difficult conditions have deprived some of us of it. The great political novel about war, starvation, oppression and international crime organisations? That's not what I write. I write about one single individual, and the story of that single individual may be transmuted into something more, giving a possibility for greater perspectives. I don't like political correctness – at least not excessive political correctness – and that was a factor when it came to creating my police team, though I knew some people would criticise me. I tried to create a credible team with a set of characters that I like to explore. I'm equally interested in the complexity of men and women, so for me the gender of a specific character is not crucial. I hope that goes for my readers as well, as long as the character I've created is of interest. I was bored with the typical stigmatised crime novel inspector. I wanted my inspector to be amiable, friendly and an honest person – a man, what's more, without any drinking problems. Radical, I know. All that without being a superhero, of course. Similarly, with the rest of his team, I prefer not to exaggerate their characteristics, which would muddy the focus of the narrative.

'Do I write Swedish noir? Perhaps. I like to feel I write about… life.'

Another Bergman

Marlaine Delargy talked to me about the UK publication of the first Sebastian Bergman novel (by **Michael Hjorth & Hans Rosenfeldt**) earlier than planned due to the Swedish TV series of two stories being shown on BBC4. Publication was originally meant to be January 2013, but the first novel is now out as a TV tie-in called simply, *Sebastian Bergman*, with Rolf Lassgård and the four other principal cast members featured on the cover. 'It was interesting,' noted Delargy, 'to see how a four or five hundred page novel is adapted to fit a 90-minute TV slot, particularly in the light of Ian Rankin's recent wry comments on Nordic Noir getting so much screen time. *The Killing*, *The Bridge* and *Borgen* were all written for television rather than being adapted from novels, which makes a huge difference. The writers can allow their characters the time to develop, and can introduce several plot lines which may or may not lead the audience astray. In the case of Sebastian Bergman, entire strands and characters were removed from the TV adaptation, but I think it worked equally well. It means that anyone who reads the novel after seeing the TV programme will have a different experience, but I don't think that's necessarily a bad thing. Henning Mankell's Wallander novels have undergone significant changes in the Kenneth Branagh incarnation. Sebastian himself is possibly even less appealing in the books; Rolf Lassgård's personal charisma brought a great deal to the part, which was written with him in mind. His contribution is acknowledged in the afterword to the second novel.'

The Killer's Art: Mari Jungstedt

The talented Stockholm-based author of the Inspector Knutas series may not initially appear to be different from many of her confrères in a concern for the vagaries of modern living and the compromised corruption of modern society, but **Mari Jungstedt's** approach is unusual: fragmentary, sometimes impressionistic but always delivering a caustic picture of the world we all live in. Her favoured setting of the island of Gotland suggests a congruence with the equally atmospheric writing of fellow Swede Johan Theorin. However, Jungstedt hews more closely to the police procedural format in such books as *The Killer's Art* (2010), in which a mutilated body, stripped naked, is discovered hanging by the feet in a picturesque port town. Inspector Knutas is initially stymied in his investigation, but begins to find dark revelations in the upscale world of art dealers and their moneyed clients. Jungstedt told me that she is particularly interested in reinvigorating some of the classic crime fiction motifs such as the much-explored – and possibly exhausted – locked room scenario. But like Nordic colleagues (including Camilla Läckberg), who similarly ring the changes on familiar themes, Jungstedt is always looking for a way to strip-mine such notions to refract a cold-eyed vision of modern society. (She is particularly cutting about the dumbing-down of modern broadcast media.) These concerns are at the heart of such books as *The Dangerous Game* (set in the fashion industry), as is a preoccupation with the way in which human beings treat each other. Like Charles Dickens, with whom she would otherwise appear to have very little in common, Jungstedt sometimes appears to be making an indirect plea for all of us simply to behave better towards each other.

Out of the Chrysalis

Why isn't she better known? **Pernille Rygg** may not have made the kind of breakthrough in the UK that many of her colleagues have, but that's not because of any lack of literary clout on her part – or because of inadequate translations. (Although the latter have comprehensively sunk several other talented writers to whom justice was not done.) Rygg was the recipient of highly accomplished renderings into English by the late Joan Tate, who in her day was one of the most visible translators of Scandinavian fiction. (Unfortunately, however, this was before the real Nordic crime wave had achieved the juggernaut proportions it now possesses.) Two of Rygg's books deserve close attention, the finely-honed *The Butterfly Effect* (first published in 1995 and appearing in Britain in 2004) and *The Golden Section* (1997 and 2003 respectively), with a vividly realised Oslo matching the books' sheer narrative gusto.

Look Back in Anger

Attention must be paid to the quirky writing of **Stefan Tegenfalk**, a Stockholm-born novelist whose uncompromising *Anger Mode* (2009) inaugurated a muscular trilogy about the tough and unsentimental detective, Walter Gröhn of the Stockholm police. A particular speciality of the writer is his extremely astringent treatment of his villains, often worthy of the American master Elmore Leonard.

The French View

The writer **Sean French** (one half of the English duo which writes as 'Nicci French', along with his wife Nicci Gerrard) is himself half-Swedish, and told me of his interest in the Scandicrime wave. 'This explosion of talent really is a phenomenon. Of course, success breeds success (like all the tennis players who followed Bjorn Borg), but I think there's more to it than that. The history of Sweden (especially, though it applies to the other Scandinavian countries as well) in the twentieth century really is extraordinary. It went from extreme poverty (at one time a third of the population emigrated to America) to being virtually the most prosperous country in the world, and unlike the US, this was achieved with consensus, social cohesion and the most effective welfare state the world had ever seen. I've sometimes felt in Sweden that it was what the Soviet Union would have been like if Communism had worked.

'I feel that this amazing change left a feeling of unease – that beneath all the prosperity, something was wrong, that there was a price to pay. This was partly almost a psychic wound – that the material success hid a sort of spiritual emptiness. And it was political as well. There was much murkiness about the Swedish miracle: it benefitted hugely while being neutral in two world wars while at the same time being a major manufacturer of arms. (Bofors – home of the Bofors gun – is just up the road from where we live.) There was strong sympathy for Nazi Germany before and during the Second World War in many parts of Swedish society. I remember being shocked when I read Ingmar Bergman's autobiography, in which he said that for the whole of the war he wanted Germany to win.

'And obviously there were the ten thrillers of Sjöwall & Wahlöö, which really set it off. I think many fans of Henning Mankell don't realise the extent to which Wallander is a reworking (to put it kindly) of Martin Beck. And the radical, almost paranoid politics of Stieg Larsson were clearly anticipated by Sjöwall & Wahlöö's radical sense of political betrayal at the highest level of Swedish society.

'One other thought,' continued French, 'there was always a great passion in Scandinavia for the Golden Age detective stories of Agatha Christie and Dorothy L. Sayers. I suspect that one of the attractions of many Scandinavian thriller writers is that they take the intricate, almost artificial plots of Christie and Sayers and put them in pungent, realistic settings. (One of the Sjöwall & Wahlöö books is actually called *The Locked Room*.)'

Reality beckons

'I wonder if fantasy crime isn't a nearly exhausted genre,' **Anna Paterson** said speculatively. Anna, a writer and translator from the Germanic languages, told me she believes that one trend in crime fiction is to move closer to documented reality. 'One example: **Set Mattson's** *The Price of Evil* (*Ondskanpris* 2012), a police procedural in a carefully researched historical setting (May 1945 to December 1946, when Malmö received 1000s of refugees, many just released from concentration and extermination camps). Then there is *The Case of Thomas Quick: How to Create a Serial Killer*, a meticulous compilation, in semi-fictional form, of the life and court convictions of a notorious serial killer and/or mythomaniac. The work (*Fallet Thomas Quick. Att skapa en seriemördare*, 2012) is written by **Hannes Råstam**, an investigative journalist who died in January 2012. The book has been enthusiastically received by many, including crime writer and criminology professor Leif GW Persson, who has written the foreword. There are other straws in the wind, including *The Spring Tide* (*Springfloden*, 2012), the first book by **Cilla and Rolf Börjlind**, both skilled scriptwriters. The crime, a brutal murder, is a closed case. Twenty years later, the documentation is seen as a suitable research topic for a police academy student, who unravels its secrets.'

5: The New King: Jo Nesbo and Other Norwegians

Norse Quartet

There are a slew of trenchant native writers, but Norwegian crime might be said to have four principal points of interest: the snatching of Stieg Larsson's crown by **Jo Nesbo** and his cult Norwegian copper Harry Hole; the much-acclaimed **Karin Fossum's** nuanced, Rendellian evocation of Nordic society; the remarkable private eye outings of **Gunnar Staalesen** (with pleasing echoes of such American writers as Ross Macdonald); and the growing cult success of the acerbic novels of **Thomas Enger.**

Uneasy Lies the Head

For many foreigners, Norway remains the most visually impressive of the Scandinavian countries. That is hardly surprising given the trips visitors have taken across the fjords – trips which include the most awe-inspiring vistas one may witness anywhere in the world. But as any Norwegian will tell you, whether we sample such natural beauty or experience the more quotidian elements of life in Oslo, we have actually seen a mere fraction of this remarkable country. The greatest concentration of population is, inevitably, in Oslo, but one should not forget that there are Norwegians spread out among the vast expanses of the country away from its more populous areas. As well as reminding you of such facts, the patriotic Norwegian will remind you of the country's imperishable cultural history, which is (in terms of its influence) considerable. Drama, for instance, after the titanic example of Henrik Ibsen, was never the same, with a far more penetrating examination of the psychological states of characters (and the *mauvais foi* in which so many of us live) than dramatists had previously attempted. (The exception perhaps, was Shakespeare but the Norwegian writer was very much of the modern world.) And in the twenty-first century, the astonishing achievement of the painter Edvard Munch is now widely considered to be among the most considerable of any artist – and, like Ibsen, his is very much a vision of the modern world, a postlapsarian view of modern life which takes in the dark and uncompromising psychology of the two dramatists. In political terms, Norwegians (until recently) have adopted a realpolitik as their view of the world in which they live, with less sense of division than might be encountered in either Britain or America. But if there are fissures in the Norwegian vision of the world, it is the country's crime writers (as much as politicians or pundits) who have anatomised such things in a dispassionate (but committed) fashion. Endemic corruption is often a pervasive presence in the crime fiction emanating from Norway, given more prominence than it might have in the real world in order to serve a narrative function – crime fiction, after all, needs its villains.

To some degree, all notable success in the arts (both popular and serious) are both self-fulfilling and self-replicating, and – above all – omnivorous. This was very much the case with the success of Scandinavian crime fiction, and readers quickly proved to be voraciously hungry for new writers who would provide the same fascination as those they had already encountered. If they had enjoyed novels featuring such characters as Kurt Wallander and Lisbeth Salander, what other writers could they turn to who would supply the same incidental pleasures? The syndrome is hardly a new one: the success of the work of Charles Dickens quickly led to a host of other writers ploughing the same furrow. The Norwegian writer, of course, writes in nothing like the style of Stieg Larsson, and, although both men favour international, globe-trotting scenarios in their books, Nesbo's fictional universe is markedly different from that of his late Swedish confrère. But in one incontrovertible area at least, Nesbo has inherited the Larsson crown: phenomenal, jaw-dropping sales. Other publishers may have described their own Scandinavian buy-ins as The Next SL, but that is usually said more in hope than expectation; Jo's success is a world away from that of his nearest living rivals, and shows no signs whatsoever of flagging.

How do you say...?

I first met Nesbo several years ago (long before his megastar status) at a meal given to celebrate the UK translation of one of his books, and noticed that, as the wine flowed, the English and American guests around the table were anglicising both his name and that of his recovering alcoholic detective, Harry Hole. When I tentatively suggested that perhaps we should be calling Jo something like 'Yerr Nesbur' and his detective 'Harry Hurler', he gave a wry smile and replied: 'Well, strictly speaking, yes – but you're not Scandinavians, and we learn to accept that our names will have... interesting pronunciations abroad.'

Ironically, with the belated issue of Nesbo's first Harry Hole novel *The Bat* in the UK in 2012, readers will be amused to discover that jokes about the mispronunciation of the protagonist's names abound (the Australian coppers Harry works with in the book mostly call him 'Harry Holy'). But *The Bat* is not the book with which English and American readers first discovered Nesbo. Books such as *The Devil's Star* (2003), the lacerating *The Redbreast* (2000) and, more recently, the massively successful *The Snowman* (2010), established Nesbo as one of the most trenchant and idiosyncratic writers of modern crime fiction. Inevitably, of course, his formidable narrative skills have made him a sure-fire ringer-of-tills. It's interesting to note that an index of this success (in the UK at least) is the fact that certain market book stalls throughout the country have stock that consists of just one solitary writer, such is their level of popularity. It used to be the English writer Martina Cole; now it's the Norwegian Jo Nesbo who fills the entire stall. But Nesbo's appeal may also be attributed to the fact that his books appear to communicate salient, caustic facts about modern society, giving them a kind of added value alongside their considerable expertise as pieces of literary entertainment. By describing the sometimes seismic changes in

Scandinavian society, Nesbo is perceived as throwing a spotlight on the dangerous, conflicted world of contemporary society; and his books address unpalatable truths about aspects of society that are not being tackled in anything but crime fiction.

The Protean Mr Nesbo

The composer and lyricist Steven Sondheim has a line about 'careering from career to career', a notion that may well have been created for Jo Nesbo. As an athletic teenager, he made an auspicious debut in the Norwegian Premier League football team Molde, his mind full of dreams about playing for Tottenham Hotspur in England (the latter is still a team he follows). But catastrophe struck: he ripped the ligaments in both his knees, and was obliged to cast around for another way to earn his living. This second career was to provide his first taste of humongous success. As a musician, he was in a rock band, called 'Di Derre' (roughly: 'Them There'), which enjoyed healthy stints at the top of the Norwegian charts. The band's second album was a bestseller for several years. Nesbo's skills also extended to the financial arena, but readers have cause to be grateful to a long-haul flight which had Nesbo struggling over a book he had been commissioned to write (and had little enthusiasm for) about life on the road for a rock musician. Instead of writing about drugs and sexually available young women, he decided to try his hand at fiction and wrote a detective novel, submitting it pseudonymously (fearing that it would be rejected as 'another crap book by a rock star'). That novel was *The Bat Man* (1997), and had nothing to do with Bob Kane and Bill Finger's vengeful Dark Knight – a fact emphasised in the 2012 British publication which dropped the word 'Man'.

The Bat

There is a nigh-legendary lost Lon Chaney silent film, *London After Midnight*, which has become the Holy Grail for film collectors. All that still exist are several fascinating stills, and film aficionados yearn for the day when a copy turns up in someone's garage. Hopes, however, are fading in the twenty-first century, as such a piece of serendipity is beginning to seem increasingly unlikely. But something vaguely similar has happened for English-speaking admirers of the most commercially successful of all current Scandinavian crime writers, Jo Nesbo. While British and American readers had long taken the writer's dogged alcoholic detective Harry Hole to their hearts and followed his alternatingly brilliant and shambolic career through a series of books, there was one appearance by the detective accessible only to those who read Norwegian or other Scandinavian languages: Harry's first appearance in a book called *The Bat Man*. It was perhaps inevitable that with the megaselling success of such recent Nesbo novels as *The Snowman* (optioned by Martin Scorsese) that the writer's product-hungry UK publishers would belatedly dust off this earlier book for our delectation (Harry had first come to the attention of UK readers with a later adventure, *The Devil's Star*). And so, finally, that first novel was published, translated by Nesbo's customary English alter ego, Don Bartlett (something of a star in his own right), with a variety of Scandinavian writers beating a path to his door (as discussed later).

Hole in the Chronology

The book is now simply called *The Bat*. No doubt this is to avoid confusion with a certain Dark Knight of Gotham City – although Nesbo has told me that he was indeed influenced by the graphic novels writer Frank Miller, who turned Batman into an ageing semi-fascist bruiser. And now that we finally have the opportunity to read this debut novel, does it turn out to be a fledgling effort which would have best been left untranslated? Or does it fill in gaps in the Harry Hole chronology that will be eagerly fallen upon by Nesbo admirers?

The first thing to strike the reader about *The Bat* is that what appeared to be the internationalism of recent Nesbo novels (plumping Harry down into such locations as Hong Kong, far away from his standard stamping ground of Oslo) is actually not a new phenomenon. This first book transplants an uneasy Harry to a quirkily realised Australia, and pairs him up with a sardonic Aboriginal cop, Andrew. And if this suggests multiple crime fiction clichés already folded into Nesbo's work (cop as fish-out-of-water, ill-matched squabbling police duo), well – yes, there is no denying that these are familiar tropes. But in this very first book Nesbo is already taking on clichés, ruthlessly tearing apart and reinventing them (something, in fact, that he has said he enjoyed in the writing of Frank Miller in the latter's graphic novel *Sin City*). As Harry tracks down the murderer of a young Norwegian woman, a minor TV star reduced to living in desperate circumstances, he is already fully formed as the difficult, vulnerable but counterintuitive personality we have come to know. His growing, awkward relationship with a young Swedish barmaid in Sydney is wonderfully handled. As are the various elements of culture shock: Harry is always a strange object to his Australian colleagues, and the evocation of Australia itself has the customary Nesbo expertise (there is perhaps, a slightly surreal quality for the British reader as Harry is constantly going from Paddington to King's Cross to Oxford Street, providing a reminder that the Antipodes appropriated quite a few place names from the mother country). What's also apparent in this first book is Nesbo's reluctance to artificially boost the excitement of his steadily-unfolding narrative – the first violent action happens some distance into the book and has the usual realistic acceptance of just what violence does to the human body (here, Harry's dental work). The novel also contains some particularly polished writing – one wonders how much to credit Bartlett for this, who has Harry describing people as rather British 'arseholes' rather than the standard US 'assholes'. But the most satisfying aspect of *The Bat* is that we can now see the organic shape that Nesbo's work was always intended to take, and the canvas stretching out in front of us is a particularly crowded one.

Giving the Devil His Due

English-speaking readers, however, were first treated to *The Devil's Star* in 2005 (two years after its appearance in its original language) and instantly took the troubled, wry Norwegian copper Harry Hole to their hearts, warts and all. That book, set during a heatwave which has the residents of Oslo suffering, begins with a woman discovering small black lumps in her cooking. It is, in fact, congealed blood dripping from a body in the flat above (right from the start of his career, Nesbo has demonstrated a gift for the unpleasant but plausible detail). Chief of Police Møller is reluctant to call upon the best detective he has, Harry Hole, as the latter's dependence on the bottle has made him unreliable. He assigns detective Tom Waaler to work with his erratic star policeman, but Harry is to discover that Tom is not all that he seems – and may have some involvement with the murder of a colleague. The body in the attic flat, a naked young woman whose corpse has been mutilated, has a pentagram discovered beneath her eyelid. As well as the sharply observed grotesque detail, always a Nesbo speciality, we're given a picture of a police force stretched to its limits and a society struggling to deal with seismic change – although all of this is couched in storytelling of the first order. Interestingly – for those aware of such things – another stellar career was being brought to our attention with this book, that of the translator Don Bartlett, who has proved to be a notable linguistic alter ego of Jo Nesbo over the years. (He has also fulfilled the same function for other masters such as Gunnar Staalesen, discussed separately.) Just a few pages of Bartlett's rendering of Nesbo's prose demonstrates why several writers are prepared to queue up – and even wait some considerable time – to be translated by this ace practitioner of his craft.

In 2005, Nesbo delivered one of his most chilling and provocative novels with *The Redeemer*. The book begins in Oslo in Christmas (after his peripatetic wanderings, Harry is now firmly in his home territory) where a crowd of shoppers are listening to a Salvation Army band, when one of the musicians is shot and killed. It's a crime without motive and without logic, and Harry and his colleagues are stymied – until it becomes clear that the victim was the wrong man, and a variety of clues (credit cards, passport) point to a professional assassin. But as Harry and co. close in on him, the latter's desperation makes him ever more dangerous. By now, readers had become accustomed to the fact that Nesbo's novels tackled serious issues along with the pulse-raising exigencies of the thriller, and taken on board here are the chaos at the desperate bottom ends of society, the often malign influence of religion and the limits of human responsibility.

Pressing the Buttons

Similarly, *Nemesis* (in another exemplary translation by Don Bartlett) pushed the customary thriller buttons (the book begins with an explosive bank robbery) while focusing on the demands of character: Harry's drunken sexual tryst with an ex-girlfriend ends with her death, while Harry has no memory of the events leading up to this catastrophe. Then he begins to receive a series of threatening e-mails. Along with all this, intriguingly, there were indications in the book that Nesbo's career was moving in a different direction – a direction that has sometimes proved controversial. His novels were becoming bigger and more ambitious, but it could hardly be argued that the new international focus (to blossom in full with the next novel) was something new in the writer's work – after all, the very first Harry Hole novel had his detective in a foreign country. But with *The Snowman* (2010) there was a noticeable finessing of aspects of Nesbo's strategies: a more ambitious reach and a more obvious relationship with the commercial blockbuster thriller. But any feelings that the sharp individual character of the earlier books was becoming diluted in the process were swept away by the astonishing success of the book, which proved to be the novel which incontrovertibly placed Nesbo at the very top of the tree in terms of Scandinavian crime fiction sales. Its gruesome, bloodcurdling plot begins with a young boy discovering a snowman in the garden, its eyes positioned to gaze into a bedroom window and (around its neck) his mother's scarf. The image was intensely cinematic (perhaps it is the aspect which attracted the director Martin Scorsese), but Nesbo – as ever – refuses to neglect the importance of characterisation, with Harry dealing with a difficult new female partner, Katrine Bratt, even as he finds himself up against an evil of an almost cosmic level.

Not di Lampedusa

The following book, *The Leopard* (2011), however, was more coolly received, with Nesbo admirers wondering if the writer needed to recharge his batteries. *The Leopard* is always engaging, but lacks the intensity of most of the writer's work. What's more, the internationalism of the narrative seems more bolted on. However, the book proved to be something of a blip, as its successor, *Phantom* (2012), demonstrated unequivocally that Nesbo had lost none of his considerable skills. Its enthusiastic reception was shored up by the subsequent appearance (also in 2012) of the first Harry Hole novel in translation in the UK, *The Bat*, discussed earlier. Briony Everroad, of Nesbo's UK publishers Harvill Secker, told me she noted a shift in reader patterns, led by the Scandinavians. 'Scandinavian crime fiction is still extremely popular in today's market,' she said, 'and this is good news not only for crime readers but also for the dissemination of translated fiction more generally. I see it as a sign that readers are becoming more adventurous, and this encourages publishers to seek new talent from different shores. There is something exotic about the inhospitable climate and the darkness in Scandinavia, but even if readers are drawn to the stories for this reason, they swiftly discover that they are well written, engaging novels that hold their own against their English-language counterparts. Jo Nesbo's readership is an excellent example of this adventurous spirit at work. His fan base continues to grow as readers delve into his world of tightly plotted thrillers set (mostly) in wintry Oslo, and what they discover along the way is the essential humanity of the troubled protagonist Harry. And despite the accelerated pace, the books are also profoundly moving.'

Uncrowned Crime Queen of Norway: Karin Fossum

In the Darkness is, in some ways, the perfect approach to **Karin Fossum's** dark, minatory world, in which the levels of psychological acuity are set against a stunningly executed narrative. What's more, the particular interest of the book to Fossum aficionados is that this is the first novel to feature Inspector Sejer, her iconic sleuth figure. A woman is strolling by the river one afternoon when a corpse floats to the surface of the cold water. She instructs her daughter to wait while she contacts the police, but in the phone booth, the woman, Eva, dials another number... The dead man, Egil, has been missing for some months, and it isn't long before the flinty Inspector Sejer and his team find themselves on the trail of a violent murderer. But it's an ineluctably cold trail, and proves just as puzzling as another case on the Inspector's crowded desk – that of a murdered prostitute found dead just before the man in the river went missing. But then the woman who discovered the body, Eva, receives a phone call in the middle of the night. It is a phone call which is to set in train a terrifying series of events.

There is a piquant comparison here with the first Jo Nesbo novel featuring his copper Harry Hole, also belatedly appearing in the UK in 2012 as *The Bat*. This first novel for English-speaking readers featuring Fossum's signature character Sejer shares with the Nesbo book one thing: there is no sense of a tyro effort in which boundaries are being tested – as with her fellow Norwegian, everything arrives fully realised from Fossum and has all the authority that we have come to expect from the later books. And it's hardly surprising to note that her British publisher chose an encomium from Nesbo calling Fossum a 'truly great writer'. As ever with Fossum, one is reminded (pleasurably) of two other female explorers of the darker reaches of the psyche, one American and one British: Patricia Highsmith and Ruth Rendell.

Don't Mess with Hanne

As ex-minister of justice for her country, the forthright **Anne Holt** hardly paints a roseate view of Denmark's urban areas and outer reaches in her novels. *1222* has a classic isolated, Christie-style setting for its mayhem, but *The Blind Goddess* may be a better starting point for those new to her work. Holt is one of Scandinavia's most popular crime authors. Her interesting succession of careers began in the Oslo Police Department, and she subsequently founded her own law firm. She was then appointed to government and served as Norway's Minister for Justice between 1996 and 1997. Her first book was published in 1993 and she has since developed two sequences: the Hanne Wilhelmsen series and the Johanne Vik series, both of which will be published in English by Corvus. Holt has sold over five million copies and her books have been translated into twenty-five languages. She is the recipient of several international awards including Riverton Prize (*Rivertonprisen*), the Booksellers' Prize (*Bokhandlerprisen*) and was nominated for the 2011 Edgar Award.

Blind Justice

It would be a touch unfair to single out one British publisher for the out-of-sequence appearance of Scandinavian crime fiction in translation: many writers have been on the receiving end of this syndrome, notably Håkan Nesser (who is characteristically wry about the experience) and the Norwegian star author, Anne Holt. With Jo Nesbo's first novel *The Bat*, as discussed earlier, filling in gaps in the early life of his copper Harry Hole (though we've got to know Harry pretty thoroughly from subsequent books), we now also have the opportunity – in *The Blind Goddess* – to acquaint ourselves with the very first appearance of Anne Holt's tough lesbian policewoman, Hanne Wilhelmsen, even though we already know her as the paralysed heroine of the much later *1222* (an energetic reworking of the Golden Age-style 'secluded location' mystery).

In this first book, which took a jaw-dropping 19 years to reach the UK (in a translation by the much-revered Tom Geddes), Hanne is a youthful detective, still possessing the use of her legs and pounding the streets of Oslo. On the outskirts of the city, the body of a murdered drug dealer is discovered by Karin Borg, a corporate lawyer out for a morning run. The face of the corpse has been cut away – but it appears that the murderer is to be discovered quickly: a student, drenched in blood, staggers through the streets of the city. He is arrested, but remains silent. When he finally speaks, it is apparent that he is not Norwegian – and to everyone's surprise, he requests that the woman who discovered the body, Karin Borg, should represent him. Assigned to the case are lawyer Håkan Sand and Inspector Hanne Wilhelmsen, a woman used to getting results. But things quickly become complicated by more murders and a high-profile criminal lawyer offering to take the case of the suspect (who is now identified as Dutch) away from Karin Borg. And there are some very dangerous people – both in drug-trafficking circles and in the city's most influential coteries – who have a keen interest in keeping dark matters unilluminated.

A corollary effect of reading Anne Holt's Hanne Wilhelmsen chronicles out of sequence is a necessary adjustment of our expectations. The later *1222* came across very much as a twentieth-century reinvention of Christie-style motifs (a tactic also used by another Nordic noir star, Camilla Läckberg), but this first book is constructed much more along the lines of a tough police procedural in the vein of such writers as Ed McBain – though it's none the worse for that. The protagonist's sexuality, present but hardly emphasised in the later book, is here more clearly identified, and the difficulties in keeping her private life private provide an added level of interest in *The Blind Goddess*. Perhaps the passage of two decades since the novel was written have rendered it less contemporary (one wonders if the Norwegian police force is quite as unenlightened regarding women in the twenty-first century), but this is a fascinating piece to slot into the puzzle that is the work of Anne Holt. There are a slew of other novels still to be translated, and readers will be grateful for them – in whatever order they appear.

Norwegian Noir: Thomas Enger

In terms of its crime fiction, Norway has undoubtedly punched above its weight, with fewer writers from that country than from Sweden entering the fray, but all the Norwegian talents have made highly individual (and markedly differentiated) contributions to the field. (The accomplished Norwegian crime writers **Thorkild**

Damhaug and **Chris Tvedt** both received the prestigious Riverton Award.) But a breakthrough in the UK, sadly, does not come to all writers. It did, however, come to one deserving crime scribe. The ascent of **Thomas Enger** – both in terms of critical approbation and sales – has been swift, but it is no more than the talented Enger deserves. With his first novel to appear in English, *Burned* (2010), Enger determinedly set out his stall as a confrontational and edgy writer. But perhaps his most signal achievement was in the creation of an unorthodox and unusual hero in the physically scarred journalist Henning Juul. And given the Nordic countries' tricky relationship with religious fundamentalism, the positioning of this theme at the heart of the novel was a particularly interesting strategy. (The book was blessed with a notably copacetic translation by Charlotte Barslund.) The central murder case of the book is built around what appears to be a Sharia-type religious killing in present-day Norway, and in the obsessive, conflicted hero (carrying the scars he obtained in a fire), Enger has created one of the most memorable journalist/protagonists in the crime field; and that is no easy task – it's a profession that has been sorely (and lazily) overrepresented in the genre.

Enger on Enger

I spoke to the quietly-spoken, likable Enger on one of his visits to this country, and discovered that he felt a certain dichotomy between the comfortable, well-heeled society that he (and his central character) live in – and the fact that many Norwegians do not feel at ease with this privileged lifestyle. But the sense of personal responsibility that Enger touches upon is something he has infused into his driven hero, and in both *Burned* and its caustic successor, *Pierced* (2012), it grants the grimly compelling narrative a solid underpinning of seriousness (but never at the expense of keeping the readers turning the pages). Where the author particularly excels is in his refusal to grant an easy answer to many of the difficult social problems raised in the books – Enger is not the kind of a writer to adopt such a facile strategy. Walking from a meal at the

Norwegian ambassador's residence (passing a noisy demonstration outside the Israeli embassy, ironically by ultra-orthodox Jews protesting against the freedoms being given to women in Israel), he told me that he realises he is part of a long line of crime writers for whom social commitment is a crucial part of the armoury. (Jo Nesbo and Henning Mankell are, he said, lodestones for him.) However, Enger is always aware that an overlay of crudely freighted-in social commitment may have a deadening effect on the sheer readability of his work, and keeps such things in careful balance.

Enger said to me that *Burned* and *Pierced* had presented different challenges to him. '*Burned* is significant for me,' he said, 'as I had spent so many years trying to become an author – and the fact that I never quit, despite moments of doubt in which I might have given up on myself – and that I finally "made it" as an author with *Burned*, is something that I can (in all modesty) regard as my greatest achievement. Hopefully, that book sets up the whole Henning Juul series quite effectively. After the success I had with *Burned* (which was immensely gratifying), I guess you can imagine what kind of pressure I was under when it came to writing the next novel in the series, *Pierced*. Many publishers from all over the world had already purchased it, film production companies were fighting for the rights to make a movie out of *all* the Henning Juul novels – novels (dauntingly) I hadn't even written yet. That pressure creates a completely different writing process. You sit down nervously at the computer knowing that the words you are going to write eventually will have currency in Britain or America. Norway, after all, is a population of just five million. All of a sudden, I could reach people all over the world. I knew I had to write something really striking. And that kind of weight of expectation, of course, can get to you.

'I'm not going to tell you that it didn't intimidate me, because it did – but not to the extent that it suffocated me. I didn't lose any sleep over it. And although I hit a few bumps (which author doesn't?), I managed to work my way through it. I am really, really proud of that, especially since before I started this whole project, I was keen to progress as an author with each book. With *Pierced* I know I have. And that, I feel, is also the case with *Scarred*, the third novel in the Henning Juul series.' I asked Enger if other authors had inspired him.

'I could easily say I was inspired by *The Snowman* by Jo Nesbo, because I think that's his best book; at least it's the one that grabbed me the most. But for me, the choice of the novel that really stands out, when I look back on all the novels I have read of contemporary Scandinavian authors, is easy. *One Step Behind* by Henning Mankell. I remember picking up this novel at Heathrow when I was travelling to Mexico some hundred and twenty years ago. It was my first Mankell novel, and I didn't realise that it was even possible to write a crime novel so chilling and haunting. It was so well crafted, and I was a little sad when my airplane landed in Mexico City 11 hours later. I wanted to carry on reading. And it made me rush out and buy every other Mankell novel I could find when I got back to Norway. Because of that experience, he became a great influence on me when I tried to become an author – I wanted to become as good a writer as Mankell was. And still is.'

British Perceptions

For the British reader, it is the strange dislocation between society in the UK and that in the Scandinavian countries which is particularly piquant. (Thomas Enger has noted that there is far less perception of the world being a very dangerous place for children in the Scandinavian countries than in the UK – and the freedom granted to children by Norwegian parents might be seen as irresponsible in Britain.) Like many of his countrymen and women, Enger is well aware that social democracy in Norway has not delivered that perfect society free of crime or social injustice, but accepts that this is the world in which we all must live. His explanation for foreign fascination with Nordic Noir? 'It's the fact that we continue to be surprised by the cracks in "exemplary" societies', he says. 'The eruption of violence, for instance, somehow seems more shocking in this more carefully controlled setting.'

My Choices: KO Dahl

The veteran writer **KO Dahl** has watched views of his work shift strikingly: from early approbation in the Nordic territories (and relative disinterest in the UK) to much more international respect – though, as he told me, the appearance of his books in Britain has not always met with his approval. 'In the UK, my novels have been published in wrong order – something I know has happened with several of my colleagues,' said Dahl. 'I have written several books after those published in Britain, but one has to accept such vagaries. I'm never entirely satisfied with my work – I'm pleased, of course, that readers find things to enjoy in them, but I can always see their weaknesses all too clearly. *Lethal Investments* (1993) I'm content with; it still seems to me to have introduced the protagonist in a strong fashion, and I'm still happy with the way I handled the theme of economic crime. *The Fourth Man* (2005) is a solid noir story, in the sense that an encounter between a man and a girl provides the starting point for a crime which involves a conspiracy against the central character. *The Man in the Window* (2001) is written in a more generic 'whodunit' style. I wanted to write about familial jealousy, and also about the Second World War in a contemporary novel – both of these aspects I think I managed to realise with some success. These three books would be my own choices from my work.

'There are a great many Scandinavian novels that are not yet translated; of these my number one favourite story would be a Norwegian book written in the thirties by a writer named **Arthur Omre**. The title is *Flukten* (*The Escape*) – for me it remains one of the first and best noir stories written in Norway. And there is no getting way from the inescapable influence of Sjöwall & Wahlöö. For me, one of their best books is *The Laughing Policeman*. I would not have written it exactly as they did, I think, but it is indubitably a classic – and it is also a book that can be read over and over again.'

Thieftaker Turned Storyteller

It was in Cologne rather than Norway that I met the amiable (if physically imposing and solidly built) Norwegian writer **Jørn Lier Horst**. Over a daunting breakfast (at Fruh Bierkeller) of black pudding sausage with Bratwurst, we talk about Horst's novels featuring Chief Inspector William Wisting, which take place in Larvik, a small town with 45,000 residents located 85 miles south of Oslo. 'It's actually the place in Norway that has the most blissfully sunny days,' he says, 'in contrast to the darkness of my books.' Horst (the prize-winning author of *Dregs*) knows this territory as a detective chief superintendent, and has transmuted his experience as an investigator to give his novels the ring of authenticity. 'My job allows me to go behind police barricades, and examine how serious crime leaves residues and traces.' He looks wistfully out of the window at the rain that has just begun to fall on cobbled strasse. 'The weather preoccupies you British, doesn't it?' asks Horst. 'But', he smiles, 'it is also a default topic of conversation for many Scandinavians. The biting cold – and the drizzling rain – of Nordic crime is something that Brits feel quite at home with – less so our clear, better-ordered towns and cities (unless you live in, say, Harrogate or Cheltenham).' We talk about how the pristine environment of many Norwegian towns (leaving aside those cities with less inviting areas where immigrants are obliged to live) that have been the scene of multiple literary homicides are not really natural frameworks for crime narratives.

More appropriate, perhaps is Horst's dangerous metropolitan Larvik region. He promises to show me the area – and I promise the same to him for London. 'I'd have to say that I am most pleased with the novel *Closed for Winter* (published in 2011 in Norway, it will be published in 2013 by Sandstone Press in the UK). I don't think I'm alone in this opinion, since I won a Booksellers' Prize for it, as it was the book the Norwegian booksellers thought was the best book that year. The novel is set in Larvik, on the south-east coast of Norway, and the story opens at the end of the summer season, at the beginning of autumn, when the nights are drawing in and the mists come swirling in from the sea. The summer visitors have gone, and the summer cottages are being shut up for the winter. This bleak setting takes on a sense of unease and fear as the first murder victim is discovered. The sinister atmosphere is heightened by the mysterious phenomenon of dead birds dropping from the sky. I tried to write something with a special dense atmosphere that makes it a story that creeps under the skin of the reader. It is, I hope, a book in which the drama is as much in the mood and the environment, as in the mystery and action.'

I ask Horst about his views on the work of his colleagues. 'Well, I am seldom jealous of other writers. But to find a book where I envy the writer, I'd have to go over 40 years back in time, to Maj Sjöwall and Per Wahlöö. With their ten books about Martin Beck they created a new genre – and all those who came after them are in their debt – including me. I particularly like the third book in the series, *The Man on the Balcony*, perhaps because this is where we are introduced to one of my favourite characters – the boorish detective Gunvald Larsson. The story is quietly told, with subtle characterisations and interesting small syncopes – deliberately missing elements which are particularly intriguing. It is also a novel that creates a sense of dissonance and anxiety in the reader.'

Bloody Bergen

Bergen may be a beautiful city, but it has its less salubrious side – and **Gunnar Staalesen**'s volatile detective Varg Veum knows every inch of it. But it was in Hamburg that I met the urbane Norwegian master Staalesen, author of such accomplished novels as *The Writing on the Wall*. We'd met several times in London, and he'd proved to be extremely civilised company. As we strolled through the historic goose market, he talked about his recent royal encounter: it was Staalesen – something of a Norwegian celebrity – who showed Prince Charles and the Duchess of Cornwall around on a visit to Norway. He constantly reminds us that he is one of the finest Nordic novelists with such books as *The Consorts of Death* (2009), the 13th novel in the series about his Bergen sleuth Varg Veum. Staalesen strives to extirpate the parochial in his writing, describing himself as a Norwegian writer of detective novels, but working within an international genre, and drawing on a variety of writers from other countries to recharge his creative batteries (always, above all, he says, 'the inestimable American Ross Macdonald'). Nature is a key element for his writing (as it is, he says, in most Norwegian novels, be they detective or mainstream fiction). 'Regarding a sense of place,' he said, 'it is imperative for me to draw a precise picture of my stamping ground: the second largest city in Norway, Bergen. It's a rainy city, which ensures that it is the perfect background for my type of *noir*, private eye stories. Rainswept streets are a satisfying ingredient in this field.'

St Mary Mead in Norway

Norway continues to produce intriguing writing in the crime field, not all of it edgy and violent (though the latter genre remains the norm). As the nonpareil translator **Kari Dickson** said to me: 'One Norwegian crime writer I've read recently – and really loved – is **Hans Olav Lahlum**, who writes charming, witty and slightly wry retro-crime, á la Agatha Christie.'

6: Dark Nights in Iceland and Finland

The dark, frigid nights of Iceland – and its recent dramatic history, including volcanic eruptions and financial crashes – can be seen (curiously refracted) through the work of the undisputed King and Queen of Icelandic crime fiction, **Yrsa Sigurdardóttir** and the masterly **Arnaldur Indridason**, winner of a prestigious CWA Dagger Award for his novel *Silence of the Grave* (2001), with pronounced social concerns important in both of the duo's books. And the relatively modest number of Icelandic writers making their mark may increase shortly; an upcoming author of promise is **Arni Thorarinsson**, already gleaning praise from such equally talented contemporaries as **Ragnar Jónasson**. And there are other names jostling for attention… but are these writers giving us a realistic picture of their country? Homicide statistics in Iceland show that there are two or three murders committed per annum. That's one of the lowest figures in the world, and in itself a sign that the country is a safe and peaceful country to live in. Personally, though, I'm quite happy to enter the darker universe of Icelandic crime fiction – where life is cheaper than in the real world.

A Brit in Iceland

Quentin Bates is a British writer who sets his adroitly written mysteries in Iceland, a county he has many connections with (not least by marriage). A discussion with him is instructive regarding his second home. 'The Icelanders aren't here yet,' he told me. 'We English-language readers have seen the Swedes and the Norwegians so far, and the Danes in the shape of Sara Blædel, Kaaberbol & Friis, Leif Davidsen and the mighty Jussi Adler-Olsen are appearing on the scene, but so far Iceland and Finland are underrepresented, at least in English translation.

'In fact,' he continues, 'it's odd that it seems to be such a battle for Nordic crime writers to reach English, considering the pool of talent that's out there. It's difficult to tell if this is a reflection on British (and US) readers who haven't traditionally been keen on translated fiction, or if this is a reflection on British (and American) publishers who haven't been keen to take a chance on translated stuff that they don't believe will sell. Whatever the reasoning, the Swedes (Stieg Larsson, Henning Mankell) and the Norwegians (Jo Nesbo et al) have laid that myth to rest, especially with something of a headlong rush to sign up Swedish writers once Stieg Larsson had shown what could be done.'

So where are the Icelanders with their jaw-cracking names and odd letters that nobody knows how to pronounce? Arnaldur Indriðason and Yrsa Sigurdardóttir have been solid sellers for some years already. It was only in 2012 that **Viktor Arnar Ingólfsson's** intriguing *The Flatey Enigma* was published in English by Amazon-Crossing. He has two more impressive books to his credit: *The House of Evidence* and *Daybreak*. **Árni Thórarinsson's** *The Season of the Witch*, chronicles one of the journalist Einar's assignments. It's also interesting to note that a newcomer to publishing, AmazonCrossing imprint, rather than an established publisher, is taking the gamble on these two authors in English. Yrsa and Arnaldur have been in and out of bestseller lists for a good many years already – notably in Germany.

Icelanders

Bates notes that one of the quirks of Icelandic is that people don't tend to have surnames. The patronymic -sson or -dóttir isn't, in fact, a name. It tells someone whose child you are, but a person's proper name is the given name. Even the current Prime Minister would be properly addressed simply as Jóhanna, so using first names (as above) isn't over-familiarity. 'In fact,' says Bates, 'several Icelandic authors who have never been seen in English have been stalwarts of

European publishers' lists for years, mainly in German and French. Viktor Arnar Ingólfsson and Árni Thorarinsson are not youngsters. Both have been writing for a great many years and have impressive backlists, and both have been published abroad; Viktor Arnar in German and Árni in both French and German translations. There are other writers with these strong backlists. **Stefán Máni** is available in French and German. **Thráinn Bertelsson**, film director and currently maverick MP is also published in German, as are books by **Ævar Örn Jósepsson**, **Lilja Sigurdardóttir** and the mysterious **Stella Blómkvist** (who bucks the trend by having a surname, although this is a pseudonym for an as-yet-unidentified public figure in Iceland, and speculation has been rife over the years as to his or her real identity). The oddball **Hallgrímur Helgason** has made it into English as well as German, but his brand of quirky experimental fiction that breaks rules and plays fast and loose with established boundaries doesn't sit too comfortably within the thriller/crime bracket. Then there are the young guns that German publishers have already been quick to pick up. Former journalist **Óskar Hrafn Thorvaldsson**'s *Martröð Millanna* (*The Millionaires' Nightmare*) has been well received in Germany and radio journalist, musician and translator **Jón Hallur Stefánsson**'s *Krosstré* is in German *as Eiskalte Stille* (*Icy Cold Stillness*). The old guard will continue to pump them out. Yrsa and Arnaldur aren't going to go away. Stefán Máni and Ævar Örn Jósepsson have dedicated followings, as do Viktor ArnarIngólfsson and Árni Thorarinsson. But perhaps the real talents to watch out for are **Ottar Norðfjörð** and **Ragnar Jónasson**, as I'd say that they have staying power to stick with this genre.'

Bates, however, doesn't mince words. 'There are plenty of other Icelandic crime writers there who haven't been picked up by German or other publishers – possibly with good reason. Icelandic publishers don't edit heavily, nowhere near as rigorously as British or American publishers do. Arnaldur's first book *Sons of the Dust* was pretty rough; it sold only a few hundred copies and was never translated. I'm not sure he'd want to see it translated now. Also, Iceland is a small place, with a population roughly the size of Croydon's. Arnaldur is a real rarity as a writer who doesn't have a day job of some kind.

Also, because the place is so small and there are relatively few publishers (although still rather a lot on a per capita basis – certainly more than there are in Croydon), there isn't space for a class of literary agents. Publishers act as their authors' agents in dealing with overseas publishers, and not all of them have the international contacts and expertise to do that. While Iceland has a deep literary tradition, there has been something of a suspicion of crime fiction as being not quite "proper" literature that has recently been dispelled as Iceland is currently awash with crime writers jostling for space. The success of Yrsa and Arnaldur abroad has undoubtedly been one of the main reasons behind this, along with the apparent eagerness of German, French, Spanish, Czech and Nordic publishers to seek out Icelandic crime writers as fresh talent and serious players in the present wave of Nordic crime fiction. The mystery is why English-language publishers haven't been quicker to cotton on to this as well.' Bates, perhaps, is modest about the 'Nordic Pretenders', foreigners who successfully traverse Icelandic territory: Michael Ridpath, Jan Costin Wagner, James Thompson – and Bates himself.

Body Parts and Jars: Arnaldur Indriđason

As an introduction to **Arnaldur Indriđason's** melancholy detective, Erlendur, *Hypothermia* would be hard to beat – despite, or perhaps because of – the book's glacial (in every sense) accoutrements. Erlendur becomes involved with the unofficial investigation into what appears to be the suicide of a young woman, who has hanged herself after bouts of depression. The haunted landscape of the book – haunted both physically and emotionally – mixes in various elements such as the recordings of a séance at which the dead girl was present, and the disappearance of two young people three decades earlier. It also focuses, most tellingly, on Erlendur's mission to find the body of his own brother, who died in a storm many years earlier. Erlendur struggles with his own parlous equilibrium, but arrives professionally at an awkward but persuasive conclusion. The book is one of the finest by a truly incisive writer.

While a variety of writers have attempted (with great Icelandic politeness) to wrest the crown from the King of Icelandic crime fiction, Arnaldur Indriðason, the bauble on his head remains firmly in place with *Jar City* (2000) and *Black Skies* (2009), demonstrating his continuing authority in the field. As in such earlier novels as *The Draining Lake* and *Silence of the Grave*, Indriðason once again demonstrates his casual command of the field, with a novel set in a hubristic, pre-crash Iceland. A man fashions a crude leather mask with an iron spike fixed in the middle of the forehead. The object is, in fact, a death mask once utilised by Icelandic farmers to slaughter calves, but the forger of the mask has one overwhelming notion in mind: revenge. Indriðason's long-term protagonist, and Erlendur's colleague, Sigurdur Óli, is experiencing one of his periodic disillusionments with life in the police force after a school reunion. Iceland's current economic boom brings him no pleasure, as his personal life is in shards (with a relationship coming to a bitter end), and even his professional life is in trouble when he unwisely agrees to call on a couple of blackmailers as a favour to a friend, walking in just as a woman is savagely beaten. The woman dies, and Óli finds himself in the middle of a murder investigation. While we're given the usual comprehensive, sharply-etched picture of Reykjavík (from its elegant boardrooms to its most dispiriting slums), there is a new attention to the varieties of human experience – always a favourite subject of the author, but here laid out in a truly ambitious panoply. What is most revelatory is the fact that Indriðason's vision of human nature may initially appear to be drowning in misanthropy, but the resilience of the human spirit is never far away. And the handling of Óli's personal tribulations has considerable emotional heft. And if Indriðason is The King, the Queen is...

Dark Days with Yrsa

If you should be foolish enough to question **Yrsa Sigurdardóttir's** status as the Queen of the Icelandic crime thriller, a few pages of a typical novel – such as *The Day is Dark* – should disabuse you of any doubts. All contact has been lost with two Icelanders who have been working in an unforgiving and remote area on the north-east coast of Greenland. Yrsa Sigurdardóttir's long-term protagonist, Thóra Gudmundsdóttir, is hired to investigate, and begins to wonder whether there is any connection with a woman who disappeared from the inhospitable site several months earlier. Her investigations are hardly helped by the implacable hostility of the few locals – and Thóra begins to wonder if one of the team at the site may have some involvement with the disappearance. As always with this highly accomplished writer, it is the surefire combination of elements which makes *The Day is Dark* work so well – the beautifully characterised Thóra (one of the most distinctive protagonists in modern day crime fiction) and the atmosphere of a frigid climate in which the residue of deadly human malfeasance is never far away. But as with all the best books by Yrsa Sigurdardóttir, it is the constant presence of nameless, imminent threat which ensures that the narrative hold here is absolutely unbreakable. Not for the first time, one is reminded that Sigurdardóttir has much in common with horror writers, where the same sense of danger results in that pleasurable rising of the hackles on the back of the neck. Sigurdardóttir remains the undisputed queen of the Icelandic thriller. A disturbing 2012 novel, *I Remember You*, has had an almost seismic effect on is original Icelandic readership, with its reputation as the most unsettling book the author has ever written even extending to people who find the very packaging (featuring a pair of piercing eyes) deeply unsettling – all, inevitably, grist to the sales mill. In *I Remember You*, Sigurdardóttir draws on the heritage of Icelandic literature, channelling ancient folk tales and ghost stories into a vision of modern Icelandic society, with the country's financial upheavals feeding the novel's violent strategies. Film rights were bought by much-respected producer Sigurjon Sighvatsson, who won the Palm d'Or for David Lynch's *Wild at Heart*.

Icelandic Pretenders

Is King Arnaldur looking to his laurels? There is a young pretender beavering away, his eye on the crown: **Ragnar Jónasson**, an Icelander becoming familiar to Brits for his frequent visits to the UK (he is a noted Anglophile, and the translator into Icelandic of a slew of novels by Agatha Christie). Winter in a small, isolated fishing town in the northernmost part of Iceland, only accessible via a small mountain tunnel. A young woman is found lying in the snow, half naked, bleeding and unconscious. An old writer falls to his death in the local theatre. A young police officer, new in town, must distinguish between truth and lies, while uncovering hidden crimes of the past, in a community where he can trust no one. And there are the constant snowstorms and the 24-hour darkness to increase the pressure. Jónasson's atmospheric *Snowblind* is set in the small Icelandic town of Siglufjord, the northernmost town in the country, best known for its status in the past as the centre of herring fishing. Siglufjord now has a much smaller population than during the peak of the herring-era and can be a cold, dark and snowy place during the winter. This is a town where 'nothing ever happens', as the local police inspector puts it, but he's wrong. During the height of winter the inhabitants of Siglufjord have to endure 24 hours of darkness. The novel mostly takes place in January 2009, and the Icelandic banking crisis and the protests in downtown Reykjavik, which took place in January that year, are also stirred into the brew.

Sitting in a Thameside restaurant I asked Jónasson which of his own books he would suggest as a starting point. He muses for a minute or two. 'Being put on the spot, I would probably have to pick my second crime novel, *Snowblind*, as that was my first book to be published outside of Iceland – in Germany in 2011. It's not yet available in English. The book is also personally important to me as it is the first in a series set in the northernmost town in Iceland, Siglufjord, where my father was born and where my grandparents lived for most of their lives, Siglufjord is a very isolated town – in the dead of winter, you're under a blanket of heavy snow with no sunlight at all, but in the summertime the sun almost never sets. So an ideal setting for crime stories, of course.'

Uncharted Territory

Mention should be made of the Faroe Islands, which is almost uncharted territory in crime fiction terms. There are only 50,000 or so people in the Faroes, and precious little crime. There is also relatively little translated Faroese literature in general, and the islands' solitary crime fiction writer, **Jógvan Isaksen**, has only been translated into a few Danish and Icelandic editions. In fact, he has been writing for the best part of two decades alongside his day job as a lecturer in literature at the University of Copenhagen, with a prolific output that includes around a dozen crime stories featuring detective/journalist Hannis Martinsson between 1990 and the present, starting with *Gentle is a Summer Night in the Faroes*, a tale of brutal murder and Nazi gold.

Finnish Duo: One

Matti Joensuu's unrelenting *The Priest of Evil* was a signature novel for the late writer, whose books were always keenly focused. Joensuu's stamping ground is Finland – and specifically Helsinki. That city is perhaps less frequented than other Scandinavian crime spots, and Matti Joensuu is the perfect conduit to Finland's less welcoming alleys – and more stygian psychological states. But Finland is still to some degree crime-writing terra incognita, so I asked one of my crime-reviewing confrères, Peter Rozovsky, if anything Finnish had taken his fancy.

'If I wanted the money, I'd like to have written *The Girl with the Dragon Tattoo*,' he replied. 'If I wanted the thrill of high artistic accomplishment and the respect of posterity, I'd like to have written anything by Maj Sjöwall and Per Wahlöö. But since I'm a reader, and an impatient critic with a taste for novelty, I'd mention a more recent book (at least in its English version): **Harri Nykänen's** *Raid and the Blackest Sheep*. It's a Finnish novel that is not only chock-full of the deadpan humour that delights me so much when it breaks through Nordic crime fiction's reputation for dour moral rectitude, it actually revels in it, going beyond even what the puckish Nykänen achieves in his other work translated into English. *Raid and the Blackest Sheep* is all deadpan, all the time. How about this passage, in which Nykänen somehow imparts a touch of gentle, even affecting looniness to a racist conspiracy theorist of a police officer: "Kempas once had a nightmare that hundreds of sprightly little gypsy children had rained down from the sky, and immediately upon landing, they scampered about causing all kinds of mischief. But for every one he caught, a fresh bunch of sneering faces appeared. While in the sauna at a seminar on white-collar crime, having drunk a few beers and several shots, he had divulged the nightmare to some co-workers. They could barely breathe from laughing until they realised the dream was based on a genuine fear."

'It helps, perhaps, that the book is a crime novel only incidentally. Raid, a hit man, takes on the unusual job of driving an old gangster home to die. Along the way, Raid and the old gangster settle scores of several kinds, police on their trail, including an officer sympathetic to Raid. They do so, however, in a loose, episodic fashion that is more *Pickwick Papers* than *Death Wish*. Not only that, but everyone – Raid, the old man (Nygren), the sympathetic Helsinki detective Jansson – turns introspective even as he observes the outside world. "An object has no value without a story," the old man explains as he and Raid set out, "and there's a good one behind this lighter, It gives it a reason for being." Nygren patted the back seat. "This car too has a story. And this coat... and this watch." Deadpan road story? Mortality tale? Social critique? Take your pick. If you pick up *Raid and the Blackest Sheep*, just don't expect a typical detective story.'

Finnish Duo: Two

Matti Joensuu died in 2011, and that loss immediately weakened the hold that the already tenuous field of Finnish crime fiction had on the genre. *Priest of Evil* (2006) had been a notably impressive novel that enjoyed much critical favour. The writer was keen to tackle areas largely avoided by other writers (such as crimes committed by children). But Joensuu's death does not cut Finland loose from the current Nordic wave; another (younger) Finnish writer of note is **Kjell Westö**. His novels (written in Swedish – he is a Finland-Swede) have a distinct and individual character with *Lang* (2005) fusing elements of eroticism into its sardonic tale of contemporary Helsinki. There are elements of Hitchcock in the writer's work in the sense that ordinary individuals can be capable of the most appalling acts, given the right (or wrong) circumstances.

Not Quite Götterdämmerung

Jan Costin Wagner is a significant figure in Finnish crime fiction literature, although he was not himself born in that country. He is, in fact, a native of Germany, as his surname might suggest. Wagner parlayed his skills as a journalist into a series of lean and austere books such as *Ice Moon* (2006) and the elusive, slightly mystifying *The Winter of the Lions* (2009), featuring his police copper Kimmo Joentaa. This is a series that has taken an oblique approach to delineating the psychology of its characters. The writer's quietly despairing *Silence* (2010) has gleaned Germany's major crime fiction prize.

7: Darkness in Denmark

Smilla's Significance

The unprecedented success of the Danish TV series *The Killing* has established the country as a key location for Nordic Noir, but its literary legacy is quite as formidable. A major current star of the genre has been signalled by the worldwide acclaim for Danish crime king **Jussi Adler-Olsen**; the writer began as more of a *succès d'estime* in the UK, but his sales are catching up with his prodigious European figures. He is a writer who trades in several of the pressing themes and issues that engage Denmark's crime scribes. But pre Adler-Olsen, Denmark – as a country – could claim one triumph that is crucially significant in modern crime fiction. Perhaps the real progenitor of the new Scandinavian wave is one book: **Peter Høeg**'s atmospheric *Miss Smilla's Feeling for Snow* (1992). Massively influential, Høeg's subtle and allusive novel inaugurated the current Scandinavian crime wave and sets its counterintuitive heroine among the snowbound wastes of Jämtland.

Jussi Adler-Olsen: The Unyielding View

Who are the Pheasant Killers? In **Jussi Adler-Olsen's** book, *Disgrace* (2008, translated by Kyle Semmel), these men are the well-educated, extremely privileged leaders of society (whose leisure activities include the game-shooting suggested by the original Danish title – the book was rejigged as *Disgrace* in the UK to chime with the single word title sequence established by the author's earlier *Mercy*, 2007). These supercilious individuals (given to calling each other 'old boy') sport a withering contempt for those without 'proper fortunes'; and consider that the ruling class is at its best when hunting and killing. But before British readers decide that Adler-Olsen has the British Cabinet in his sights for this novel, it is necessary to remind oneself that the setting here is Denmark, however much these characters may have an English resonance. It has to be said, however, that the old Etonians who rule Britain, however jaundiced our views of them, are not the despicable types that the Pheasant Killers are in Adler-Olsen's book. While perhaps sharing the sybaritic superciliousness, the Danish movers and shakers targeted in *Disgrace* are actually psychopaths, concealing violent crimes. They are so thoroughly nasty (as characterised by their creator) that the author has perhaps made something of a rod for his own back. Is it really credible that these monsters (led by the utterly ruthless captain of industry and sexual abuser, Ditlev Pram), having concealed a brutal killing in the past, can continue with the kind of murderous clandestine activities we are told about and yet still maintain their position in society?

But those who enjoyed the compelling and astringent *Mercy* will be pleased to know that we are back in the lively company of Adler-Olsen's signature characters: his acerbic copper Carl Mørck, still in the police graveyard shift of Department Q (which to the frustration of his superiors he has managed to transform into a successful facility), and his eccentric Muslim assistant Assad. Assad is nominally a cleaner, but is more like Mørck's Watson (or, indeed, his Holmes, as Assad is capable of brilliant counterintuitive deductions, and totally lacks interpersonal skills; most of the humour in the book comes from Assad's inelegant bluntness). Against all the odds (and executive hopes that they will simply fester in their barely-regarded department), Mørck and Assad cracked the case of a missing politician in the earlier *Mercy*, so expectations for them are now minimally higher. *Disgrace* is as weighty and imposing as its predecessor (running to 500 pages), and despite the depredations of its loathsome villains, it is, strangely, not as dark as the earlier book – possibly because there is not quite an equivalent for the desperate sympathy we felt for the tortured female politician in *Mercy*. But at the centre of *Disgrace* is another tormented woman, and she is perhaps the most successful element of the new book. Kimmie lives on the fringes of society in a hidden subterranean room that only she has access to. She's a strange mixture, with characteristics of both the homeless (passers-by remark on her rank odour) and a higher social bracket – she can transform herself into a more soignée figure, and is, in fact, a wealthy heiress living rough after the psychological trauma of the murder she took part in years earlier with Ditlev Pram. And despite the fact that a fall guy has been provided for the killing, her well-heeled ex-friends know that Kimmie could bring about their downfall. The suspense here is whether or not the antisocial Mørck and his maladroit assistant can find her before she is silenced permanently.

Some might recognise the influence of the English writer Len Deighton in this book – the sardonic dialogue and the resolutely unromantic surroundings in which the central characters work owe not a little to the dingy office life of Deighton's nameless spy. There is a real skill in the handling of the triple narrative: the desperate, off-the-radar life of the disturbed Kimmie (whose only friend is a heroin-addicted prostitute), the search by the idiosyncratic police duo and the parallel pursuit by the villainous plutocrats. But some may have reservations about the latter – the mystery element of the earlier book is dispensed with, as we are party to the activities of Ditlev Pram and his vicious colleagues right from the start of the book. What's more, Adler-Olsen has decided to allow his villains no nuance; as characters they are simply irredeemably evil and their function is rudimentary. This makes the experience of reading *Disgrace* less complex and challenging than its predecessor, but there is no questioning the iron grip the author maintains on the reader, which is quite as unshakeable as that of the earlier book.

The Danish Crime Queen

Few would argue that a key position is held in Danish crime fiction by the charismatic and engaging **Sara Blaedel** whose raven-tressed image adorns bookshop windows all over Germany and Sweden. Her extremely popular, crisply-written crime series is set down in what is now recognised as a 'Copenhagen Noir' style, a style which has earned her pole position in the field. 'I always endeavour to freight in elements of edginess and social awareness in my novels,' she told me. Blaedel won the Danish Crime Academy Award for her debut in 2004 with *Green Dust*; and her heroine, Detective Inspector Louise Rick, also featured in *Call Me Princess*, one of her books to enjoy an English translation. (In 2012, Blaedel was signed by a different UK publisher for a more aggressive attempt to break her work in the UK.) On a visit to Denmark, I asked her which of her books she felt came closest to her original vision. 'I suppose,' she replied, 'I'm most proud of *Farewell to Freedom* (*Aldrig Mere Fri*). When my characters Louise Rick and Camilla Lind first came into my life, I did not really anticipate that our association would be as long-lasting and deep as it has been. As each character has grown and developed, they have encountered certain key turning points that have influenced all of their subsequent experiences. Many of these important moments and events happen in that book.

'And *Farewell to Freedom* is truly a Copenhagen story, set on the beloved streets and boulevards I have known so intimately my entire life. I worked hard to capture the nuances of Copenhagen's neighbourhoods and bring them to life for readers. And the book also afforded me the opportunity to learn a great deal about human trafficking, and the horrors encountered by its victims. While this is a side of the human experience we might all wish did not exist, regrettably, it does, and I believe that shining a light on it is the best means we have of combating it. Parts of the novel are also drawn from experiences I had as a reporter covering the former Yugoslavia; these had a deep and abiding impact on me. As a reader, I have most enjoyed the books by the Swedish author Åsa Larsson. Her stories keep me absolutely rapt, and I look forward to each new title. Because my goal is to create characters that spring to life on the page, I greatly admire what Åsa has done in this area with her protagonist Rebecka Martinsson.'

I talked to Sara Blaedel's UK editor, Jade Chandler, after a books-related event she and I did with Yrsa Sigurdardóttir at the inaugural Bloody Scotland crime festival. 'Finding out about authors whose work is not originally published in English is the biggest barrier to British publishers discovering gems of the genre like Sara Blaedel,' said Chandler. 'In Sara's case, I was very lucky that she had recently found a US publisher, Pegasus, with whom Sphere shares another Scandinavian author, Hans Koppel. Simply being published by Pegasus was in itself a great recommendation and also meant that I was able to read Sara's first two novels in English before making the decision to move ahead with publishing her on the Sphere list. One of the great attractions of Sara's novels (such as *Blue Blood*, the new UK title for *Call Me Princess*) is their lead protagonist, Detective Louise Rick. Here we have a strong female lead who brings to mind hugely popular Scandinavian TV detectives like *The Killing*'s Sarah Lund and *The Bridge*'s Saga Noren. Of course, the fashion for female leads in crime fiction is not just restricted to TV, and I'm sure the trend owes a lot to the stellar success of Stieg Larsson's Lisbeth Salander in the *Millennium* trilogy. It is notable, however, that five out of the six novels on the shortlist for 2012's Theakstons Old Peculier Crime Novel of the Year Award featured female protagonists; it looks as though the female lead has now become a cornerstone of the genre. In Sara's novels, Louise Rick is supported in each story by her equally likeable best friend, journalist Camilla Lind, a friendship that allows Louise to go about solving cases with her usual panache, whilst retaining a common human touch that is framed perfectly by the friendship between the two women. The explosion of Scandinavian crime fiction in the last few years has meant that readers who might previously have been intimidated by translated novels are no longer put off by such things. Nowadays, a novelist like Sara will be enjoyed by someone who is also a fan of English language crime novelists such as Karin Slaughter, for example, rather than someone who is looking exclusively for crime in translation. To my mind, this marks a huge breakthrough in terms of broadening the market from what had previously been seen as a niche area to something that has successfully been absorbed into the mainstream.'

Invisible Murder

The first book to reach the UK from the duo of **Lene Kaaberbøl** and **Agnete Friis**, *The Boy in the Suitcase*, immediately established them as markedly different from most other purveyors of Scandinavian crime fiction. With highly successful individual careers as a fantasy writer (Lene) and children's writer (Agnete), it was perhaps inevitable that their joint efforts would be somewhat different from those of their contemporaries – and so it proved to be with that first book, a thoroughly involving outing for their do-gooding protagonist Nina Borg. And if the adjective just used for the team's nurse heroine sounds off-putting, it should be borne in mind that Nina is a fully rounded character, with her almost obsessive altruistic notions treated in a critical and clear-eyed fashion by her creators. (Kaaberbol and Friis themselves, however, carry the customary baggage of a keen desire to change society for the better – *de rigueur* for writers of Nordic noir, it seems. Is it a legal requirement?)

The second book to appear in English translation by Kaaberbøl and Friis, the poetically titled *Invisible Murder*, demonstrated that the duo were not one-hit wonders. If anything, this second outing for the vulnerable (if, at times, annoying) Nina is more impressive than its predecessor. In an abandoned Soviet military hospital in Hungary, two Roma boys are scrabbling to survive by scavenging for old supplies (and even weapons) to resell on the black market – then the boys make a truly alarming discovery. They have, in fact, lit a metaphorical touchpaper, and the events that follow are to prove potentially lethal for a great many people. Danish Red Cross nurse Nina Borg is following her usual star – helping those living at the extremes of society. In this case, the recipients of her charitable assistance are a group of Hungarian gypsies who are living clandestinely in a garage in Copenhagen. But Nina, as ever, is a woman who cannot avoid finding trouble – very much the case here, and the stakes are of the highest. As in the previous novel, there is the judicious balance of narrative momentum and carefully wrought characterisation. The reader may be reminded of the earlier novels of the English duo who comprise Nicci French; that team's books similarly put us on the side of women who make a series of mistakes – and even, at times, have the reader shouting at the page – but with whom we find ourselves ineluctably involved. The other reminiscence that may spring to mind here is, strangely, John Buchan, whose hero, Richard Hannay, loses a finger in one book. The similar shocking loss of a digit here at the book's climax shows that readers have not lost the capacity to be horrified. On the evidence of their work so far, readers will be hoping that Lene Kaaberbøl and Agnete Friis are in it for the long haul.

Serious Subjects: Leif Davidsen

The weighty, ambitious novels of **Leif Davidsen** – books that tackle serious subjects – have a keen following, with *The Woman from Bratislava* (2009) something of a high water-mark. I spoke to Davidsen about this signature novel. 'Of the books of mine which have been translated into English, I think I'm happiest with *The Woman from Bratislava*. But favourites of one's own novels? Difficult! There is too much of a Sophie's Choice notion concerning the whole idea. However, I like *The Woman from Bratislava*, because I think I succeeded in playing creatively with plot and character, with language – and with time and place. I was very much inspired by the movie *The Usual Suspects* when I wrote it. I like the relatively open ending, and I was intrigued by the way three different points of view tell basically the same story. The film deals with a subject matter which in a Danish context is both complex and repressed: secrets from the Second World War and the Cold War. My Danish readers seem to prefer *Lime's Photograph* (2001). But I'm proud of a recent (2012) book, called *My Brother's Keeper*. It is a historical novel – thriller – set in Denmark, Spain and Moscow in 1937–38. It was a dream to write, because I could combine two great interests of my life: the Spanish Civil War and Stalin's brutal regime, which in spite of its evilness, served as a role model for many intellectuals in the West. I don`t think I have ever been happier writing than when I wrote that novel. Every morning, when

I sat down at my desk I had a sensation of bliss.'

Davidsen echoes something Håkan Nesser also said to me about a key Scandinavian novel. 'I would love to have written *Miss Smilla's Feeling for Snow* by Peter Høeg, but I would have changed the ending, which I found did not work. Recently I read an interview with Peter, where he says that he purposely wrote a non-ending, because he wanted to simultaneously explore the thriller and to deconstruct the genre. I love the book because of its characters and the way Høeg slowly but surely builds the plot. His grasp of language is impressive; I love that important first sentence, and it is a wonderful read – until the last fifty pages or so. I love thrillers myself and find no reason to deconstruct them, but I do like to experiment with form and language.'

Other Danish crime fiction of note includes that of **Mikkel Birkegaard** (whose *Library of Shadows* was a striking debut, commixing notions of conspiracy and the significance of the printed word – the latter a key pride of the Danes), and the sardonic writing of **Sissel-Jo Gazan**. Gazan clearly does not share many of her countrymen's roseate view of Demark (it was once a truism that Danes considered themselves 'blessed'), preferring to live in Germany.

8: The Nordic Screen: Film and TV adaptations

The continuing success of original Scandinavian TV shows, notably *The Killing* – and filmed adaptations such as the British and Swedish Wallanders – shows no signs of abating, although both the Swedish films of the Larsson *Millennium* Trilogy and the David Fincher version of the first book have less momentum these days. The future of Nordic Noir cinema? It may have the initials 'JN': Jo Nesbo film adaptations such as *Headhunters* and *Jackpot* have won enthusiastic audiences, with Martin Scorsese scheduled to direct the film of Nesbo's novel *The Snowman*.

Wallander (Film/TV)

Murder in a Quiet City: Wallanders' Ystad

When the train drops the traveller at Ystad, and one strolls the streets of the small, picturesque bijou city with its charming, Bruges-like, multi-coloured houses, it's hard not to expect Kurt Wallander (in the person of either Krister Henriksson or Kenneth Branagh) to emerge from the police station (actually the municipal baths, cleverly rejigged) or one of his favourite drinking spots. In fact, for lovers of both the books and the multiple TV series, every landmark in the town is familiar. The actor Krister Henriksson (the favourite Wallander of most Mankell aficionados) is often seen being filmed there ('Sometimes,' an enthusiastic woman in the local tourist office told me, 'we have cars being blown up in the street without Krister even being present!'). And when I asked about Kenneth Branagh filming the British TV series in the town, the puzzled response was: 'Who?'

Wallander Times Three

When Scandinavian crime writers visit Britain and the US, one of the most familiar questions (apart from the inevitable 'Where do you get your ideas?' which is asked of crime writers of all nations) is the following: why are particular novel sequences translated and published in the wrong order outside of their native countries? (It was something of a *cause célèbre* for instance, that as late as 2012, Jo Nesbo's first novel, *The Bat Man* (1997), had not been translated into English, despite the immense success of his subsequent novels. The novel is discussed earlier. The answer, of course, is that publishers in the UK feel that (understandably enough) they know their market, and maintain their right to choose the best book to launch particular writers in this territory, even though it may be out of sequence.

A similar syndrome was noted after the television appearance of Henning Mankell's Swedish policeman Kurt Wallander, the market leader in this territory, whose incarnation by the talented actor Krister Henriksson, giving a nigh-definitive face to Mankell's creation, had made the transition from cult viewing to TV essential. Another series was to make its mark on British viewers, one featuring British actor Kenneth Branagh (more on that anon), but the first actor to assume the role – and Henning Mankell's initial choice – was the ursine, heavyset Rolf Lassgård. Ironically, the first films featuring this actor in the role, while well received in Sweden, were not to be shown in the UK until the two later incarnations mentioned above had already established a hold (the debut episode was an adaptation of *The Man who Smiled*, 2003, directed by Leif Lindblom) and British viewers, not in possession of the full facts, imagined they were seeing a replacement for Krister Henriksson. This skewed transmission order did no favours to Lassgård, whose version was a more irascible, less winning incarnation of the character, and seemed to be something of an unwelcome departure from the one British viewers were used to. Also, it has to be said, Lassgård lacked the more presentable (and initially slimmer) Henriksson's charisma. But now that the original series has been shown and has become familiar to viewers, it may finally be possible for those unconvinced by the late appearance of Lassgård to examine his performance more objectively, particularly as the actor has also now been seen in the UK as the brusque criminal profiler, Sebastian Bergman (a character who has the distinction of being the first television crime fiction protagonist as sexual predator).

Inevitably, no television version of a multifaceted character such as Kurt Wallander could do justice to the original, but all three actors who have assumed the role have managed to illuminate facets of the detective, each having an individual ring of verisimilitude. Lassgård was first in line, of course, and the comparisons that the character draws between himself and the obese TV detective in the 1970s Frank Cannon (played by the heavyweight William Conrad) drew attention to the not inconsiderable girth of the Swedish actor. But those for whom this was a major issue were forgetting that Mankell had written his character as overweight, and it was both brave and sensible to avoid prettifying the detective for a television version of the role. (It could be argued that such a process happened with Gunnar Staalesen's middle-aged private eye Varg Veum – discussed later – who had been cast with the younger, and extremely good-looking, Trond Espen Seim. Over the course of his assumption of the role, Lassgård was able to freight in a variety of understated character traits in the context of his slightly larger-than-life performance and succeeded in conveying the inner life of the character.

Henriksson Takes Over

The next actor to play the role, however, was to bring markedly different qualities to his take. Subtler and more understated than his predecessor, Krister Henriksson (a distinguished Swedish stage actor) might be said to have utilised the possibilities of the television medium in a fashion which gave more weight to certain elements in the adaptations in which he starred: a more pronounced use of observation in the role and a marked withholding of information and emotional resonance in relation to the other characters. (In this respect his performance echoed the success of Roy Marsden's similarly understated, watchful performance in the long-running series of adaptations of PD James' Adam Dalgliesh novels.) Henriksson is particularly acute in showing his character's uneasy internalisation of the variety of crises in his personal life (such as the increasingly fraught efforts to establish a relationship with his ailing father and with his resentful daughter, who feels that he has been a non-presence at most of the important events in her life).

Visit Beautiful Ystad

And more than in the previous series, Henriksson's Wallander is very much an inhabitant of the small town of Ystad, lovingly filmed by the various directors (while the production manager makes the most of the relatively few usable locations). While the real elements of the town are used creatively within the context of the television series (as they were in the subsequent Branagh adaptations) the various directors employed convey a sense of the organic relationship between the policeman and the small Scania town that is his stamping ground. (Although, as with Colin Dexter's use of Oxford in his Morse novels and the subsequent TV series, there is an unconscionably high murder and crime rate in this relatively sedate setting.) The Henriksson series, when it moved beyond the picturesque Ystad, unfolded a Sweden which was some considerable distance from the photogenic country presented in travel guides, and the sense of the flat quotidian elements of the country were conveyed in a low-key but visually appropriate fashion. (Interestingly the various directors sometimes demonstrated the Sweden that had a kinship with the unromantic, urban Italy of the mid-period films of Michelangelo Antonioni.)

Parental Dereliction

Performances throughout the series are uniformly excellent, notably that of the ill-fated actress Johanna Sällström as Wallander's equally confrontational daughter, particularly as her character, Linda, is shoehorned uncomfortably into the role of a policewoman working with her father. A variety of clashes between the two becomes quite as intriguing as the exigencies of the principal plot, and we, the viewers, are made to feel as keenly as Wallander himself the wish that some kind of *simpatico* relationship might be established between the father and daughter. (Although there is absolutely no doubt that Linda's criticisms of her father's dereliction of duty as a parent are justified, we are almost invariably on his side in any disputes, regarding her as stiff-necked and unbending.) Watching the episode in which Henriksson appears, following the actress's suicide after periods of depression, is a bittersweet experience, and it is very easy to understand why Henning Mankell felt that he could not continue writing about the character after Sällström's death, which affected him very deeply.

Wallander Three: The British Arrive

Yellow Bird, the company co-created by Henning Mankell in order to film the Wallander books (and which was subsequently to enjoy massive success with its films of Stieg Larsson's *Millennium* Trilogy), was involved in the production of the third series to feature the detective. This time a radically different approach was taken – one that has been controversial, but which has more recently been winning critical acclaim to match its appeal for audiences (viewing figures have always been healthy). The notion with this series was to utilise the original Swedish settings for the filming, but to cast a British actor, Kenneth Branagh, as Mankell's tenacious policeman and have dialogue in English. He was to be surrounded by a cadre of solid British character actors (including some future stars such as Tom Hiddleston, now more famous as the villainous Loki, brother and archenemy of the Marvel superhero Thor in Branagh's film of the latter). But the settings would remain authentic – an approach similarly adopted in the David Fincher film of Larsson's *The Girl with the Dragon Tattoo*. And while this approach paid tangible dividends, there was the inevitable corollary of the language/setting interface – or lack of it. The convention of the central characters speaking English rather than Swedish was handled capably until the actors were obliged to mention place names or character names which brought the whole enterprise thudding down to earth – and not just for more sophisticated multilingual viewers. Emblematic of this approach was the crass decision to mispronounce the central character's name with a soft 'W' (as opposed to the authentic Vallander). This decision was defended at a meeting of London's Nordic Noir book club when the producer, Frances Hopkinson of Left Bank Productions, after making a persuasive case for the 1960s/1970s visual accoutrements of the programme, defended the decision to anglicise the central character's name on the basis that new actors arriving on the set from the UK would find it easier to cope with.

Arcadian Settings, Anguished Attitudes

In fact, the 'British' series was made with great skill, and Branagh's approach to Wallander balanced a judicious mix of the authoritative and the troubled. Counterintuitive in his detective skills, the character occasionally seems barely able to function in a social setting, such is his alienated state. In some episodes, his colleagues are wont to stand around – in rather unlikely fashion – looking at him in dismay as he struggles to finish a coherent sentence. This very different, more histrionic approach to that of Henriksson finally pays dividends, although the focus on Wallander's personal problems shifted the narrative from the mechanics of the plot to the tormented, emotionally bruised central character. Looked at objectively, this remains a perfectly valid strategy, and Branagh frequently presented something of a masterclass in acting. However persuasive the actor was, the dedicated aficionados of Krister Henriksson's performance frequently reacted in very negative fashion, criticising Branagh for the more self-consciously 'actorly' elements of his performance. Ironically, one of the other elements of the first British series – its strikingly beautiful cinematography and Arcadian vision of Sweden, with its exquisite fields of waving wheat and chiaroscuro sunsets – while handled by the filmmakers with immense assurance, was similarly criticised for what was felt to be a prettification of the less visually sumptuous original series.

Re-evaluation

For a time, it seemed, the knives were out for this third incarnation of Henning Mankell's character, and most pundits (and those members of the audience familiar with the novels) elected the Krister Henriksson series as the definitive take on Wallander. But the British actors and production team could cheer themselves up with the fact that such criticism did not appear to be shared by viewers; the impressive audience figures that the various Branagh films enjoyed were proof of that, and there was no disputing the fact that the series was watched by a far greater audience than had tuned in to either of the earlier series. This might have been due, to some degree, to the resistance of some audiences to subtitles (it should be noted that these series appeared before the prodigious success of the Danish series *The Killing* altered British audiences' resistance to subtitled product). But something else happened in between the various seasons of the Branagh adaptations: there was a notable softening of response with some (not all) pundits more disposed to make allowances for the necessary compromises of the Branagh series and see it as a perfectly valid take on the original novels, one that might have been better received had not the authentic Krister Henriksson series blazed the trail.

British Politesse

In the final analysis though, there is a nagging sense that the British series is one obviously made by visitors to the country rather than natives of it. This might be pointed up by an examination of the two adaptations (Swedish and British) of Henning Mankell's 1994 novel *The Man who Smiled*, which illuminate and encapsulate the different approaches. The vicious industrialist who is the villain of the piece (and is involved in the illegal trafficking of organs) is – in the original series – state-sponsored and, what's more, enjoys a queasy relationship with his daughter. (In fact, she has been impregnated by him.) The state sponsorship and the incestuous insemination element were politely elided for the British remake, giving the sense that the visitors did not want to tread on any toes. This begged the question: which was most in need of excision, an incestuous relationship or Swedish state collusion with corrupt business? Such caveats aside, a persuasive case might be made for the Branagh series as a perfectly valid approach to Henning Mankell's signature character.

Channelling Bergman

Toby Haynes directed one of the most striking episodes (the premier, in fact) in the 2012 series of the Branagh Wallander series: *An Event in Autumn,* based on a Mankell short story. Speaking to Mankell, I found him effusive in his praise for the episode – and he even said that his late father-in-law might have been impressed. Mankell said he sensed a Bergman 'tone'. Accordingly, I asked the cineliterate Toby Haynes whether or not Ingmar Bergman was ever in his mind when filming. 'I'm very flattered by what Henning says about this film,' smiled Haynes. 'It doesn't get better than to have your work compared to Bergman's, but I guess it must have been a passive influence on us – through the landscape and Henning's own Bergman-esque characters – as Bergman's films themselves were not a direct point of reference for me. As a director I never felt I had to bring any additional scandic influences to the film – I kept away from the books or other TV dramas like *The Killing* or even Bergman's films. The script really spoke for itself. Peter Harness had written this tight and focused story, given it such a drive and character journey that it became my sole guide and measure. The story was firmly rooted in wintery Ystad and that dictates your tone and colour – you can't go into this trying to resist what it is, you have to dive in and absorb the world around you. We film *Wallander* entirely on location, which is a luxury most other television shows cannot afford. It was very much the producer Sanne Wohlenberg's feeling that I should go out as early as possible and really just suck in the whole landscape and the way the people operate out there. It was a great idea and the time I spent there became the backbone of my research for the project.

'Ystad is a seaside summer town so it has this sleepy feel in winter, it really seems the whole town goes to bed at 7pm. The days are short and there are these long twilight hours, and I found myself cycling around this grey-blue environment. I would often stop at the beach and stare out across the Baltic – the horizon was almost always shrouded in sea mist, giving that feeling of looking out into oblivion. It got me thinking about the Cold War, and how not so long ago I would have been staring towards an unseen enemy. I wondered if living on the frontline of this kind of paranoia had taken its toll on the Swedish psyche. It was certainly an environment that encouraged bleak contemplation. This was how I found many of the locations used in the film – for instance, where the arm washes up on beach, with its avenue of funny, optimistic, little beach huts against the grey Baltic sky; you find these images by osmosis not by forcing a preconceived vision or idea founded on other media.

'An Event in Autumn is very much a whodunit, but (as always) getting to the bottom of the mystery takes a personal toll on Wallander. During the course of it he makes mistakes and puts other people he cares about in danger – there is an inevitability to it, and by the end of it he knows this, and relinquishes himself to his tragic life. This brought to mind my only other reference for the piece, which was Roman Polanski's film Chinatown. Not only does it show how you navigate a story elegantly from one character's perspective without seeming tricksy or obvious, but it also had so many other similarities – like Wallander, Polanski's Jake Gittes is an experienced investigator, world weary and savvy, but he doesn't always make the right choices – in fact, the last three active decisions Jake makes at the end of Chinatown seal the grisly fate of Faye Dunaway's Evelyn Mulwray.

'Detective dramas are very much like dreams. Everything means something, there are no extraneous details or throwaway lines. It's like looking at the random pieces of a broken vase and watching them explode in reverse to take their true shape. The way Polanski shoots Chinatown is a lesson in film making, where he puts the camera, how he follows Jack Nicholson's every move, how he treats the violence with brutal frankness. It was my guiding light during this production and in tribute I placed three subtle Chinatown references into the film for fans of both to discover over time, but they're buried deep and it's going to take a very keen eye. The writer Robert Towne once described Polanski's ending to his script as "the tunnel at the end of the light" and I don't think he meant it as a compliment, but that is exactly what our film had to be – and I tried to sum this up with the final shot of Wallander's car driving through the woods into a composition of trees and falling snow, that could have been one of his father's "grouse" paintings – the ones he was doomed to repeat all his life, just as his son will repeat his own sad tale over and over again.'

The Girl with the Dragon Tattoo (Film/TV)
(Sweden, 2009, Niels Arden Orplev, director)

Yellow Bird Productions' inaugural film (in 2009) of a Stieg Larsson novel was, of course, *The Girl with the Dragon Tattoo,* preceded in the film's advertising by the word *Millennium.* The film was to be salutary in its approach to the adaptation process regarding the late writer's work. A judicious amount of pruning was (rightly) applied to a book so full of a slew of intensely detailed material – along with a degree of compression of the *dramatis personae* – as well as a slimming down of plot ramifications. And this brusque approach by director Niels Arden Orplev and screenwriters, Nikolai Arcel and Rasmus Heisterberg, paid dividends, not least in reinventing literary material for the film medium. There is a different approach to Larsson's novel than might have been expected – signally, a refusal to 'goose up' the material with set pieces designed primarily to thrill on a simple visceral level (an approach which was perhaps influential on the Hollywood version that followed). When action (inevitably) occurs in this first film of *The Girl with the Dragon Tattoo*, it has been (in a logical sense) honestly bought and paid for. Similarly responsibly handled here is the first sexual abuse by Salander's malign, bullying legal guardian, the advocate Burman – who forces her to perform oral sex on him – an action he pays for (along with a subsequent anal rape) by being equally violated by a coolly vengeful Salander wielding a dildo and using a tattoo needle. At no point are these sequences shot in exploitative fashion, and everything we see is at the service of the narrative. The casting of the various characters is peerless, with both Noomi Rapace and Michael Nyqvist perfectly incarnating Lisbeth Salander and Mikael Blomkvist. Rapace is uncompromising in rendering her elfin Goth anti-heroine uningratiating (to say the very least) but she is, accordingly, at every moment we see her, utterly mesmerising.

The Girl Who Played with Fire (Film/TV)
(Sweden, 2009, Daniel Alfredson, director)

Even before *The Girl with the Dragon Tattoo* had become the most successful Swedish-language film of all time, it had created a daunting challenge for the filmmakers: what approach should be taken with the second Larsson novel, *The Girl Who Played with Fire*? It employs many of the same creative team – with the actors Noomi Rapace and Michael Nyqvist keeping continuity with their earlier readings of Salander and Blomkvist. However, *The Girl Who Played with Fire* doesn't necessarily play by the rules regarding the standard approach to a second entry in a film trilogy; the film retains the important aspects of the book, but utilises a more kinetic (and leaner) narrative approach than that of the first film. A new director is on board, Daniel Alfredson, adopting a more linear approach than Niels Arden Orplev. Reflecting the book's focus on women's rights, such themes are even more central here, though there is a lessening of the inexorable, compulsive grip of the earlier film.

As with the book, the massive conspiracy against Salander (unjustly accused of three murders) is central, shored up with violent action (but to less effect than earlier). Following Larsson's lead in the original novel, Alfredson takes it for granted that the viewer will be familiar with the curious relationship between Salander and Blomkvist. No longer a sometime-sexual one, as in the first film, it is now a friendship, largely unacknowledged by her, but valued by him. The corollary of this assumption that we will know what's going on is that that viewers unfamiliar with the first film may be nonplussed by the fact that the principal characters don't encounter each other until some way into the narrative, when Lisbeth has been knocked to the ground and lies bleeding (although this late encounter has hefty emotional significance). There is a replay of the graphic sexuality of the earlier film with an unblushing lesbian lovemaking tryst between Lisbeth and her lover, Miriam Wu. Problems arise with, and are not surmounted by, the film's villains: Micke Spreitz as the formidable, nigh-invulnerable Niedermann looks for all the world like one of 007's film nemeses – and not to any great advantage. The same is true of Georgi Staykov, markedly too youthful for the malevolent Russian whose family connections are a key revelation. Staykov's unpersuasive mutilation makeup is reminiscent of low-budget indie horror films.

The Girl Who Kicked the Hornet's Nest (Film/TV)
(Sweden, 2009, Daniel Alfredson, director)

The third book by Stieg Larsson was also adapted by the production company Yellow Bird in 2009. This final *Millennium Trilogy* adaptation has echoes of Yellow Bird's original Henning Mankell *Wallander* television series: understated, oblique performances by (most of) the cast (á la *Wallander*) are the order of the day, with studiously non-picturesque, quotidian locales. This is matched by the unshowy storytelling. Of the three *Millennium* films, this is the one which most displays its antecedents as a film made for Swedish television. As in *The Girl with the Dragon Tattoo* and *The Girl Who Played with Fire* the filleting procedure performed on the source novels is incisively handled, with another improvement over Larsson's original: the rejigging of the opening chapters of the novel in which the seriously-injured, barely-conscious heroine, lying semi-comatose in a hospital bed after surgery for a bullet lodged in her head, realises that her hideous father is in the same hospital. The latter's night-time stalking of his vulnerable daughter is excised for the film, improving the narrative flow. (In the first film the removal of the copious details of financial scams and Blomkvist's unlikely number of sexual conquests has a similar effect.) In similar fashion, the subplot of the character-assassination poison-pen e-mails sent to Blomkvist's lover and colleague, Erika Berger, is changed, again advantageously.

One problematical aspect of the film is Salander's stalker, the monstrous Niedermann, whose non-human abilities stretch our quotient of belief – we expect a Roger Moore-era Bond to dispatch him (Niedermann's demise, courtesy of bikers he's crossed rather than Salander, who has nail-gunned his feet to the floor, is not shown – we hear it reported; if this avoids a sense of closure, it still makes its point). The court case in which Lisbeth is put on trial is triumphantly handed, with Daniel Alfredson taking the requisite amount of time for this set piece. (Salander's full-on courtroom entry – in outrageous, fuck-you Goth gear – is great fun.) Even more than in the previous films in the trilogy, the talented Noomi Rapace gives perhaps her most shaded and subtle reading here, and the film undoubtedly brings the trilogy to a satisfying close.

The Girl with the Dragon Tattoo (Film)
(US, 2011, David Fincher, director)

First of all: no spoilers! David Fincher's film of Larsson's *The Girl with the Dragon Tattoo* is a creditable remake/reimagining, with many impressive things that dispel any notion that it might be the usual ill-advised Hollywood remake of a non-English language film. As Salander, Rooney Mara may initially register less of an impression than the memorable Noomi Rapace – until halfway through the film, and then the actress (adopting a vaguely Swedish accent which, in contrast to Daniel Craig's received pronunciation, comes and goes) really makes her mark. Paunchy middle-aged journo Blomkvist/Craig has James Bond's abs, but (to his credit) never looks heroic – the spectre of 007 is kept firmly at bay.

There is, perhaps, a general softening: Lisbeth is more humanised than in Rapace's performance (there is a *Rain Man*-style breakthrough for this carefully established sociopathic personality), and, despite Fincher's promise that he was planning to push the envelope on this film, the violence and sexual abuse are slightly toned down from the Swedish version. The change of a key revelation works remarkably well, though it may upset purists, and the cool, desaturated palette of the cinematography is highly impressive, even if the Vanger mansion is often in stygian darkness. And a largely English cast of reliable presences provide impeccable support.

The Eagle: A Crime Odyssey (TV) (Denmark, 2004–6, Niels Arden Orplev et al, directors)

The central, eponymous character is an unstable half-Danish, half-

Icelandic copper, Hallgrimsson, whose sobriquet is 'The Eagle'; the detective is forcefully played by Jens Albinus. Written by Peter Thosboe and Mai Brostrøm, the series is unusually picaresque with investigations in various Scandinavian countries and Russia. Little seen in Britain (but winning an Emmy in the US), this is a striking and intelligent drama in which the total commitment of actors and directors is always evident; it certainly deserves a wider currency.

Jo Nesbo's Headhunters (Film) (Norway/Germany, 2011, Morten Tydlum, director)

If you don't like the idea of being manipulated by a novelist or filmmaker, then perhaps you should avoid *Jo Nesbo's Headhunters*. Written in a terse, pithy style (and translated in customarily nimble fashion by Don Bartlett), the novel concentrated on just three characters: two men, neither of them particularly likable, and a tall, soignée woman who is an object of desire for both. It's no surprise that the highly successful film adaptation gleaned such a following (it was the first of his books Nesbo allowed to be filmed), as the filmic properties of *Headhunters*, as well as making it a particularly invigorating read, provided the perfect, virtually story-boarded blueprint for a movie. After the mass killings in Oslo, Nesbo was in demand as a commentator on the psychological state of his country (he had already written about Norwegian neo-Nazis), but his first novel to appear since those traumatic events was more straightforward than, say, *The Snowman*. The film (directed by Morten Tydlum) captures that exhilarating, blackly comic mode. Yes, *Jo Nesbo's Headhunters* is admittedly lightweight, but, although none of the author's usual insight into Norway is forthcoming, a sizeable measure of sheer entertainment is on offer. And Nesboites appeared to like the change of pace.

It was one of Alfred Hitchcock's most subversive skills and one of which he was proud: cajoling us into being on the side of a corrupt protagonist – whether we wanted to or not. It's the strategy employed by Norway's most successful author in *Headhunters*, and Morten Tydlum's adroit and blackly comic film does highly entertaining justice to Nesbo in his kinetic adaptation. The diminutive Roger Brown (played with nice understatement by Aksel Hennie) is a wealthy and intelligent headhunter for a variety of corporations. But he has a secret life: he also practises a successful sideline in art theft, a vocation that helps him to maintain a splendidly appointed house and an exquisite wife, Diana (the willowy and imposing Synnøve Macody Lund). Brown finds himself in dire financial straits, and is obliged to make some serious illegal money. He burgles the home of a candidate he has lined up for a prestigious job, and suddenly things go seriously amiss. He has targeted a Rubens as a way of settling his debts, but during the robbery Brown comes across disturbing facts about his wife. The following day, an associate in the robbery is discovered dead in his car, and Roger finds himself in the sights of another kind of headhunter.

If you are a Nesbo aficionado hungry for a film featuring his damaged but sympathetic copper, Harry Hole, you will be obliged to adjust your expectations. The central character in *Headhunters* is (on first impression) an unpleasant, manipulative piece of work, and it is a measure of the filmmakers' skills that we find ourselves rooting for him. When the promised films of the novels by Nesbo featuring his saturnine detective are made which will be the version of *The Snowman* mentioned earlier, they'll be a very different kettle of fish. They will probably be imposing, lengthy dramas, but *Headhunters* makes for a more economical (and lighter) piece of work. The cinematic quality of the original novel has been successfully transmuted here in Morten Tydlum's capable hands, and it makes for a particularly invigorating cinematic experience – if (that is) you're not squeamish.

Jackpot (Film) (Norway, 2011, Magnus Martens, director)

If the police find you sitting dazed in a room surrounded by massive carnage, covered in blood and with a shotgun in your hands, your chances of proving yourself innocent are slim indeed. This is the intriguing premise of the second Jo Nesbo film (directed by Magnus Martens) to be made from work other than his signature Harry Hole novels. (This one is from an unpublished treatment, unlike its predecessor, and is cleverly marketed as being 'from a Jo Nesbo story that you've never read!'.) But is it as distinctive as *Jo Nesbo's Headhunters*?

Oscar (nicely underplayed by Kyrre Hellum) is a factory manager. He is no angel, but appears to have a tad more moral conscience than most of the men with whom he works. (One of them is distinctly reminiscent of Robert Carlyle's psychopathic character in the film of Irvine Welsh's *Trainspotting* and he's clearly a loose cannon who is going to cause trouble for everyone around him.) When Oscar and his colleagues win 1.7 million kroner on the pools, they are (initially) in rapturous mood. They do not foresee (as the audience clearly does) that murderous human greed will soon surface, with extremely bad results for everyone in the group – and we don't have to wait long for the consequences. The actual structure of the film is flashback, beginning with Oscar as the only person still alive after a bloody shoot-out at a strip club. To a quirkily characterised copper (played by Mads Ousdal) he tells his unlikely story – and the scepticism of the latter is a stand-in for our own feelings. While *Headhunters* was essentially a black comedy, it retained a serious edge that never allowed the viewer to forget the consequences of violent action. The tone here is much more straightforwardly comedic (notably regarding the disposal of severed body parts), but it's comedic on the subject of criminals falling out and murdering each other, a trope that stretches from Alexander MacKendrick's *The Ladykillers* up to the Coen Brothers' *A Simple Plan*. (The latter film may have been in Nesbo's mind when he wrote the original concept – and it was certainly in the mind of the director.) Although this is handled with sufficient brio, unlike the superior *Headhunters* (which stays in the mind long after the viewer has watched the film), *Jackpot* slips away far more quickly. Nevertheless, it's still an admirable set-up for the later, more ambitious Jo Nesbo films to follow.

The Killing (TV) (Denmark 2007-2012, Kristoffer Nyholm et al, directors)

A brief note on a show so exhaustively covered elsewhere: with the third and final season of the cult Danish crime series generating the same waves of enthusiasm as its predecessors (with those in Britain yet to see the series making apologies for this embarrassing omission to their friends), it's clear that the success of the show is a phenomenon unlike anything else that has happened for such an intelligent TV drama. But it's not just Sofie Gråbøl's memorable incarnation of the difficult, uncommunicative, Faroe Island sweater-wearing copper, Sarah Lund, that has created the massive enthusiasm. There are also the steely grip and unerring instincts of the show's producer Piv Bernth (the other key woman behind *The Killing*, whose contribution is as essential as that of Sofie Gråbøl), and – perhaps most important of all – the rich, complex and nuanced writing of Søren Sveistrup, unerringly shaking all the clichés out of the crime fiction genre like loose nails. Season Three gives Sarah Lund new challenges, but wisely allows her to remain something of an enigma (her creators have made the retaining of her mystique a central strategy).

The Bridge (TV) (Denmark, Sweden, 2011, Henrik Georgsson et al, directors)

The British taste for dramatised Scandinavian crime was piqued by *The Killing*, and, to a large degree, the momentum of this UK enthusiasm was maintained with this later cult series. Björn Stein's *The Bridge* may not have attained the heights of its predecessor, but acquired a dedicated following, not least for its infuriating but likable sociopathic heroine. The series, with one caveat, is one of the quirkiest and most intriguing entries in the field, utilising familiar themes but giving them an idiosyncratic twist. A body is discovered on the Oresund bridge between Sweden and Denmark (two bodies, in fact – in gruesome fashion, the torso and legs belong to different victims), and the ill-assorted female/male cop duo with equal jurisdiction obliged to work together on the case (one Swedish, one Danish) are wonderfully played by Sofia Helin and Kim Bodnia. Helin's eccentric Saga Norén certainly possessed the capacity to become as much of a cult figure as *The Killing's* Sara Lund – though she takes the latter's lack of interpersonal skills to almost cosmic levels, showing a hilarious inability to relate to other human beings. In this area, she makes Lisbeth Salander look like an agony aunt. Saga, for instance, takes Erica Jong's conception of the 'zipless fuck' to rarefied levels – sex for her is an itch that simply needs to be occasionally scratched, with zero emotional commitment. There is a slew of mystifying plot strands thrown up in the early episodes that will keep viewers comprehensively hooked – for instance, who was the scarred, half-dressed homeless girl who is poisoned in the second episode? Sofia Helin, an actress whose own slight facial scarring points up her own powerful appeal, balances the schizophrenic elements of her character with total understanding, while Kim Bodnia, functioning as the viewer's eyes (through which we review his eccentric partner), does quite as well with a far less showy part. The caveat? The super-intelligent, super-ingenious villain – when finally revealed – perhaps lacks the final ounce of evil charisma his character calls for, but the obfuscating, whodunit nature of the plot demands a certain low-key approach in order to deceive the viewer.

Banishing Bad Danish TV

I spoke to the personable Kim Bodnia about the success of *The Bridge* at a fairly prestigious Danish occasion – aboard the Danish royal yacht and in the presence of Queen Margareta. After Kim and I sheepishly agreed that we had both probably shaken the royal hand too vigorously, we discussed what it was about *The Bridge* which had attained such an ineluctable grip on the British. Bodnia smiled wryly: 'I really have no idea why this series was such a phenomenal success in Britain, although of course the groundwork had been laid by the earlier success of *The Killing*. I've noticed that the British – along with other nations – are now aware of an individual Danish identity when it comes to films, etc., rather than just grouping us all under the vague heading of "Scandinavia".' I put it to him that part of the success of the show is the fact that his character, Martin Rohde, offers the viewer a way of regarding the eccentric, autistic Saga Norén – he is our surrogate in the show. 'Yes, I think you're right,' he says, 'I'm there to say all the things about her embarrassing behaviour that the viewer would want to say if they were in that situation. But I'm glad that there was so much more to my character than that – I was given a lot to chew on as an actor.'

Bodnia is also pleased by the success of subtitled programmes such as this in the UK, and noticed that the British were far more ready to accept such things than, say, the Americans, who resist foreign language films. But there are other countries where his voice is not heard. 'For instance,' said Bodnia, 'in Germany there is a guy who always dubs me – so I imagine it would be a shock for German audiences to hear my actual voice.' I remind him that for many years in Italy a small, physically unprepossessing man had dubbed a succession of James Bonds – so that Sean Connery's 007 had the same voice as Timothy Dalton. 'Well, I don't really see that there's anything wrong with that,' replies Bodnia. 'Although I'm glad that in Denmark we always see British and American films with subtitles rather than in dubbed form. Perhaps that's why the average Scandinavian speaks reasonably good English!'

Before indelibly creating his character Martin in *The Bridge*, Kim Bodnia had a lengthy career in both Scandinavian (*Nightwatch*, *The Pusher*) and non-Scandinavian films – including a stint in Bollywood movies ('Although I didn't get to sing!'). He has ideas on why Scandinavian crime (particularly in his métier, the filmed variety) has taken such a hold. 'For quite a long time,' he says, 'our television drama was bad – really bad – unambitious, clichéd things. Then about the time of the Dogma movement (although they were not in fact responsible; I'm just using that as a calendar point), new filmmakers with new ideas came along, with a much more ambitious view of what crime dramas could do. Apart from anything else, it was the fact that directors and writers were brave enough to really take their time, so the characters could be developed at a realistic pace, as could the plots – without having to be shoehorned into relatively brief transmission slots. Although in Britain that had happened with the occasional show, I think it was the realisation on the part of modern British audiences that the necessary time would be taken – and intelligence respected – that resulted in the Danish and Swedish product being treated with such respect. And I'm lucky to be part of that.'

Sebastian Bergman (TV) (Sweden, 2010, Daniel Espinosa, director)

The two-part crime series *Sebastian Bergman: The Cursed One* arrived with certain hard-to-meet expectations, in the wake of several groundbreaking Scandinavian crime series. The format of two 90-minute episodes (directed by Daniel Espinosa) went against the current trend for multi-part series (but is none the worse for that), and as the prickly eponymous profiler, starred one of Sweden's most respected actors, Rolf Lassgård. The actor adopts an audacious tactic: he makes virtually no attempt to render the difficult, sexually predatory Bergman subtly likable, not even by a chink in the character's armour (although we are aware of the vulnerable humanity beyond the uningratiating exterior). For UK viewers, Lassgård had latterly become familiar as the original television Kurt Wallander (albeit non-sequentially after both the Henriksson and Branagh incarnations).

Police profiler Sebastian Bergman is shabby, unshaven and displays a distinctly non-PC approach to women; but this is no attractively dangerous seducer; he is more of a sex pest. Bergman is also a damaged individual, attempting to deal with grief over the tragic deaths of his wife and daughter in the 2004 Thailand tsunami. Returning to his home town after the death of his mother, Bergman encounters his old police colleague, Torkel, who is looking into the savage killing of a teenage boy. Bergman also discovers a letter with revelations of a family secret. He inveigles himself (in the teeth of some opposition) onto Torkel's team – with uncomfortable results for all concerned. The first episode is not just risk-taking in its refusal to elicit sympathy for its bear-like anti-hero, but keeps its narrative focus deliberately vague, while the second episode displays another kind of audacity: outrageous borrowings from the oeuvre of the writer Thomas Harris. In the final analysis, *Sebastian Bergman* is not an easy series, but it's unarguably one with the courage of its convictions.

Those Who Kill (TV) (Denmark, 2011, Kasper Barfoed et al, directors)

In Great Britain, the minority arts channel BBC4 broke such series as *The Killing*, and the very name of the channel became – slowly but surely – a byword for the best in Scandinavian crime television. So that when the rival British network ITV made its bid for the same market with *Those Who Kill*, there was some scepticism as to whether or not they could pull off a coup – after all, the film buyers of BBC4 seemed to have such areas pretty well sewn up. And, to some extent, so it proved. Although *Those Who Kill* (written by Elsebeth Egholm and others, and directed by Kasper Barfoed, Niles Nørløv Hansen and Birger Larsen) was made with skill and efficiency, it remained essentially a more conventional, by-the-numbers series (including a quotidian serial killer pursuit) than its more acclaimed bedfellows shown by BBC4. It had a difficult, unconventional blonde heroine, Katrine Ries Jensen (adroitly played by Laura Bach), on board, yes, but with minimal innovation and the parameters of conventional crime fiction series were adhered to far more closely than in series such as *The Killing*. Perhaps for this reason (rather than any satiety with the genre), the series made relatively little impact on its British outings.

Lilyhammer (TV) (Norway/US, 2011, Gier Henning Hopland et al, directors)

Once word of this very idiosyncratic series began to filter through, appetites were whetted – not least because of the presence of the actor Steve Van Zandt of *The Sopranos*, whose entertaining (and eccentric) performance as the absurdly bequiffed lieutenant of the murderous Tony Soprano was one of the particular pleasures of that cult series. In *Lilyhammer* (written by Anne Bjørnstrand and Eilif Skodvin, and directed by Gier Henning Hopland, Simen Alsvik and Lisa Marie Gamlem), Van Zandt (also famous as part of another New Jersey phenomenon – he is a musician in Bruce Springsteen's E Street band, usually with a bandanna covering that famous tonsure) is once again a mobster, but the context here could not be more different. (Van Zandt, though, gives what is essentially his *Sopranos* performance.) The actor (who believed he had left acting behind when *The Sopranos* finished in 2007) received a persuasive offer from a husband-and-wife team from Norway. The concept was bizarre but beguiling: an American gangster becomes part of a witness protection programme and ends up in the unlikely setting of picturesque Lillehammer in Norway. In fact, the original creators of the series had envisaged Van Zandt in the part, and he was quickly persuaded.

His character is Frank Tagliano, a New York gangster who has been relocated to Norway after turning state's evidence against fellow wise guys. He chooses the town of Lillehammer after becoming enamoured of it when it hosted the 1994 Winter Olympics. As might be guessed from the slightly absurd premise, the humour here is very different from the pitch-black variety to be found in *The Sopranos*, and the classic fish-out-of-water notion is played for surreal value. Like the earlier series featuring Van Zandt, the piece can be extremely self-referential (jokes about *The Godfather*, for instance), and the fact that the actor personally found the snowbound setting a truly radical change of departure is clearly reflected in his sometimes glazed-eyed performance. But just as it's clear that Van Zandt has no problem with the distinctively Norwegian character of the piece, there is no concomitant attempt to Americanise things here (the besetting sin of so many American adaptations of Scandinavian originals). What's more, the show even takes in differences between its Moslem, European and American characters. *Lilyhammer* was a prodigious hit in Norway with over 20 per cent of the country's population addicted to the show. It also avoided the indignity of an American remake with the original format (utilising subtitles) being presented to American viewers – something of an innovation. And even for those not persuaded by the show (the writing crucially lacks the sharp edge that would have made it far more distinctive, and there is a highly unlikely romantic subplot grafted on to the narrative that simply does not work), there is one ineluctable fact: it has its own quirky character, even when doing no more than sharing tropes and ideas with other film and television.

Borgen (TV) (Denmark, 2010, Mikkel Nørgaard, Annette K Olsen et al, directors)

The unprecedented success of *Borgen* in Great Britain cannot be denied, and it is invariably discussed within the context of the British obsession with all things Scandinavian. But does it belong in a book called *Nordic Noir*? In the final analysis, a case might be made for this as an intelligent, compulsively involving political thriller. (Political thrillers were clearly in the makers' minds; prominently displayed in the apartment of the investigative journalist intelligenty played by Birgitte Hjort Sørensen is a poster for the film *All The Presidents Men*, clearly a lodestone here. Director Annette K Olsen admitted as much to me on a visit to London.) But one of the most signal characteristics of the most successful Scandinavian filmed thrillers (such as *The Killing*) is the level of sophistication on offer in the treatment of politics – far more complex and nuanced than viewers are generally exposed to even in the best American and British dramas. That, of course, is crucial to the success of *Borgen* (written by, among others, Jeppe Gjervig Gram), but perhaps the real secret of its appeal is the strong and purposeful (but winningly vulnerable) woman at the centre of the drama, the new Danish Prime Minister Birgitte Nyborg Christensen, played by Sidse Babett Knudsen. As, week by week, she encounters a series of crises that she solves by impressive lateral thinking, her character – despite the power she wields – is not too far away from the policewomen faced with the daunting dilemmas in the police procedurals. But apart from the nonpareil acting (notably Knudsen and Sørensen), it's the rich and interesting portrait of a marriage under strain that humanises the drama and intriguingly plays audacious games with our expectations. (Just as we are beginning to be disbelieving, for example, of Birgitte's impossibly understanding and complacent husband – with even the couple's sex life being organised along political lines – everything begins to go interestingly wrong.) And as for the picture of a coalition government in which the component parts actively dislike each other – for some reason, that plot strand appears to have struck something of a chord in Britain. Wonder why?

Varg Veum (TV) (Norway, 2007–2012, Morten Tydlum et al, directors)

When Gunnar Staalesen replaced the quirky Chester Himes-style coppers, Dumbo and Mask-face, of his earlier books with the private eye Varg Veum, some kind of film adaptation was inevitable. The dogged Veum is a drinker (of Norwegian aquavit), and has a Marlowe-like respect/disrespect relationship with the (mostly hostile) police. He has no gun and is a product of the cultural attitudes of 1968. Veum was initially a social worker before he became a private investigator. His name is a play on a Viking era phrase, 'Vargr í veum', meaning, 'wolf in the sanctuary'– that's to say: a loner, a creature without peace.

Those addicted to the splendid crime novels of the Norwegian writer (which are by no means as popular in the UK as the quality of his work demands they should be) might be given pause by the casting of his social worker-cum-detective in this series. Was the good-looking, long-haired Viking type Trond Espen Seim (who resembles Marvel's thunder god super-hero Thor) really ideal material for the world-weary, middle-aged protagonist of the novels? In the event, this conventionally 'pretty', Hollywood-style casting is actually justified by the actor's highly successful, 'withholding' assumption of the part, in which Varg Veum's strange, warring mix of human sympathy and bloody-mindedness is perfectly captured. Production values on the series were notably high, with a genuinely cinematic feel for most of the episodes (although early entries were plagued by the consistent miscasting of key subsidiary roles). What is perhaps most mystifying is that, at the time of writing, the series has yet to find a British audience (although it is available on subtitled DVDs) – perhaps because the series appears to hew more closely (on the surface at least) to the format of orthodox detective shows, than such shows as the more iconoclastic *The Bridge*. As for the casting, Staalesen told me himself he was happy – but then Ian Rankin initially put the best possible face on the then-boyish John Hannah unhappily incarnating the first screen Rebus...

Jar City (Film) (Iceland, 2006, Baltasar Kormákur, director)

The number of Scandinavian films adapted from celebrated Nordic noir novels which have made an impact in the United Kingdom is relatively few, but in many ways *Jar City* is one of the key entries, in which the talented director, Baltasar Kormákur, finds the perfect cinematic equivalent for Arnaldur Indriðason's keenly focused novel. What's more, the film has enjoyed a certain currency, finding an audience beyond (if not too far beyond) the usual dedicated aficionados of such fare. Perhaps the most successful element here is the subtle, underplayed portrayal by Ingvar Sigurdsson of Indriðason's saturnine copper Erlendur, unearthing unpalatable secrets. Sigurdsson risks utilising a certain inexpressivity in creating the role (which is not to say that the actor himself is not capable of subtle colours in his performance – one of the reasons this works so well is the fact that he is clearly repressing those elements, allowing them to appear as highlights in a very understated performance). It's particularly refreshing that the film (from a screenplay by the director) avoids the temptation to utilise any synthetic pumping-up of tension and excitement in the manner of a Hollywood film, which would work against a steady accretion of detail on offer here. The final effect of *Jar City* is to make one wish that more of the author's novels had been adapted with this degree of success – but then in terms of the current Scandinavian wave, even Indridason's best work itself remains caviar to the general – praised by the cognoscenti, but outsold by many lesser writers.

Insomnia (Film) (Norway, 1997, Erik Skjoldbjærg, director)

The remarkable achievement of Christopher Nolan's *Dark Knight* trilogy has sent many a film aficionado back to the British director's earlier work, and (for those who need reminding of his achievement) his skills have been fully in evidence from his earliest movies, notably in his film *Insomnia* with Al Pacino; it's an intelligent and distinctive piece of work, offering a refreshing challenge to the viewer's perceptions. But despite Nolan's obvious skills, it is quite simply not as accomplished, strange and atmospheric as the earlier Norwegian version (from a screenplay by **Nikolaj Frobenius** and director Erik Skjoldbjærg), made in 1997, with Stellan Skarsgård using far less 'actorly' strategies to delineate his tormented on-the-edge detective, breaking every rule in the book while tackling a murderer who is a sort of doppelgänger of the detective himself. (The actor told me that he feels he gives quite different performances in different languages – and excellent though he is in Hollywood product, his work in the Nordic field is his real métier.) As so often with films in the Nordic Noir genre, the cool surface of the film here (from production design to mise-en-scène) is more redolent of European art cinema (more Antonioni than Bergman) than overtly commercial fare, as is the unforced, steadily unfolding investigation of the more stygian reaches of the human psyche. Apart from the mesmerising Skarsgård, slipping steadily into psychosis, there is an equally transfixing reading by Bjørn Floberg (Varg Veum's exasperated police contact in the adaptations of Gunnar Staalesen's novels) as a seriously deranged writer. And Floberg's reading makes a definite attempt to avoid the clichés when it comes to presenting the damaged, dangerous nemesis of the central character.

Pusher (Film) (Denmark, 1996, Nicolas Winding Refn, director)

Frank, a drug pusher who is making a comfortable living, ill-advisedly undertakes a massive deal with a consignment of drugs he has not paid for, and is arrested. He has managed to dispose of the drugs in a lake, but his real – and potentially lethal – problem is his supplier, to whom he owes a great deal of money. Even those who are only familiar with top drug dealers from the medium of film or the novel will be well aware that such individuals are not the kind that one should be in debt to – if it can possibly be avoided. Frank is obliged to plunge into the darkest reaches of Copenhagen's underworld to get himself off the hook. This caustic and uncompromising Danish crime drama is handled with a steely intensity by director Nicolas Winding Refn (he was later to bring the same intensity to the American film of James Sallis's *Drive*), but looked at in the twenty-first century, *Pusher*'s most interesting element is perhaps the performance (as the beleaguered Frank) by the versatile actor Kim Bodnia, now much more familiar playing a character on the right side of the law, the fish-out-of-water Danish cop working in Sweden in the cult series, *The Bridge.*

Unit 1/Rejsehldet (TV) (Denmark, 2000-4, Jørn Faurschou, Niels Arden Orplev et al., directors)

The neglect of this trenchantly made series (principally written by Peter Thorsboe and concerning a mobile taskforce which bolsters the local police in Denmark) is particularly unfortunate, given that far less authoritative crime dramas have found a ready audience in Britain and the United States. What is most celebrated here is the clear sense of purpose with which the filmmakers have shaped the sometimes intractable material, and there is nary a wasted word or scene, though the protagonists are (admittedly) cut from a familiar cloth.

The Hunters/False Trail (Films)
(Sweden, 1996 & 2011, Kjell Sundvall, director)

I found speaking to Rolf Lassgård on a visit he recently made to London for the film *False Trail* something of a salutary experience; this amiable, likeable Viking figure could not be more different from the difficult, uncommunicative coppers we know him best for. He smiled wryly when I pointed this out. 'Yes,' he said, 'I suppose British viewers know me best as Wallander or Sebastian Bergman, and some may have seen me in *The Hunters* and its 2012 sequel *False Trail*. But conflicted sleuths are only one part of my work. Yes, I tackle difficult individuals working with the police services, but I have other strings to my bow. I'm pleased by the fact that I played the mother in *Hairspray* – and one of my first appearances was as Puck in *A Midsummer Night's Dream* (although that *was* a long time ago). But I like the challenge – and a very fulfilling one – to work in films like *False Trail* with a remarkable director such as Kjell Sundvall.'

False Trail is a belated sequel to the earlier Scandinavian hit by the same director, *The Hunters* and the new film was originally called *The Hunters 2*. It is distinguished for some striking cinematography of its beautiful locales, but its principal virtues lie in the players: the reliable Lassgård, a mesmerising Peter Stormare and Annika Nordin. Despite the beauty of the settings, this is an uncompromising and unpredictable Scandinavian thriller. Fifteen years before, Erik (Lassgård) was obliged to leave the Norrland Police Department. He has subsequently become the National Murder Commission's most respected interrogator. Ordered by his boss to return to his home town to solve a savage killing, he reluctantly returns, fighting shy of destabilising memories waiting for him. Erik's nemesis is Torsten (Peter Stormare), and a grim duel of wits ensues.

Epilogue: Some Names to Watch For

When I did talking head duties for the BBC4 TV programme *Nordic Noir*, I shared screen time with knowledgeable Dane, **Jakob Stougaard-Nielsen**, of the Scandinavian Studies Department of University College London and we recently chatted about the writers I'd chosen to include in this study. Jakob approved, but added: 'There a couple of names I would think could profitably be included in an overview of Scandinavian crime. Norwegian **Kim Småge** (80s–90s, not translated, I think) should be mentioned as key to the pre-history of Norwegian and Swedish crime. The Finnish writer **Leena Lehtolainen** is often referred to approvingly in contemporary criticism regarding gender and crime (English translation is in the offing). Of the Danes: **Anders Bodelsen** (who specialised in neo-realism in the 60s–70s) could be considered to be the father of a particular socio-realist Danish crime tradition; and then there's **Dan Turell** representing the 1980s; and more recently **Gretelise Holm** and **Elsebeth Egholm** (who might be considered Danish femi-krimi writers). Regarding films, I'd add that Kjell Sundvall's *Jägarna* from 1996 should be worth a mention in approving terms'.

Top translator Don Bartlett added: 'I've noticed that the Danes talk about the "femi-krimi", novels (as mentioned by Jakob above) with a female investigator: Sara Blædel, **Gretelise Holm** and so on. By the way, Holm's books are interesting, perhaps more international than Sara Blædel's. And – yes, Elsebeth Egholm? Isn't she a rival for the Crime Queen title? She has two – connected – series running, and writes filmscripts. Oh – and, personally, I'd like to see a nod to **Torben Nielsen** for *Nineteen Red Roses...* '

Another valuable contact of mine is Nordic crime fiction expert

Simon Clarke, who suggested the following should at least receive a namecheck: 'Karin **Wahlerg** and **Anna Jansson** should be mentioned; two talented writers who have both been recently published by Stockholm Text. **Håkan Ostlundh** is popular in Sweden, and has just been published in English, while **Marie Hermanson** has enjoyed great success in that country, and she's due for an appearance in English. I'd certainly record **Camille Grebe** and **Åsa Traff** who are sisters. Their impressive *Some Kind of Peace* appeared in translation in the UK in 2012.'

Scandinavian specialist Nils Nordgren said to me: 'Finland is a problem for us all in terms of nailing its crime fiction; there are very few translations, even in the Nordic languages. I suppose we have to accept the fact that the Swedes and the Icelanders have done a more effective job of breaking into the English language crime market. In my home territory of Norway, some of the leading and most interesting crime writers of today are, sadly, not to be found in English: **Unni Lindell**, **Knut Faldbakken**, **Kurt Aust**, **Gert Nygårdshaug**, **Jan Mehlum** and a recent addition, **Torkil Damhaug**. But I'm pleased to say that **Tom Egeland** has had three of his books published in the UK and should be read by anyone interested in the genre. **Arthur More** is an unusual figure, a smuggler-turned-author. His crime novels (he also wrote mainstream books and short stories) were written in the 1930s and 1940s. And keeping that historical perspective (which we should), mention should also be made of **Sven Elvestad/Stein Riverton**, **Bernhard Borge/André Bjerke**, **Torolf Elster** and **Max Mauser** – in fact, these Norwegians were the finest (if not the most prolific) Scandinavian crime writers before Sjöwall & Wahlöö. On the Danish crime scene, attention needs to be paid to **Anders Bodelsen**, who wrote the thrice-filmed *The Silent Partner* (Christopher Plummer starred in one version) and several other crime novels over the years. He was, in fact, once considered almost as important as the sainted creators of Martin Beck in pointing out a new direction for crime writing in Scandinavia. Historically speaking, there is **Palle Rosenkrantz** who wrote in the early 1900s (one of his short stories was dramatised for *The Rivals of Sherlock Holmes* TV series, and starred John Thaw as DI Eigil Holst).

'Apart from those series which made a splash in the UK, there have been several popular Swedish made-for-TV crime dramas, including three recent ones, which have not yet reached an English audience: **Anna Jansson's** *Maria Wern*, **Liza Marklund's** *Annika Bengtsson* (also the subject of two earlier feature films) and an acclaimed series based on Arne Dahl's powerful novels. Then there's **Jan Guillou & Leif GW Persson's** *Anna Holt* (her name ironically prefiguring the Danish crime writer Anne Holt), *Beck* (based on Sjöwall & Wahlöö's characters) and **Helene Tursten's** *Irene Huss*. In Denmark from 2006–2008, audiences were given *Anna Pihl*, written by *Borgen* creator **Adam Price**. And in Norway two feature films and four serials have been made from the work of Karin Fossum, while six of **Unni Lindell's** crime novels have been made into TV serials. One might add a variety of police serials (of different accomplishment), *Fox Grønland*, *Black Money/White Lies*, *Codename Hunter* (I and II), all made by the same writer/director, **Jarl Emsell Larsen**, who is at present making another, *Eye Witness*.'(Nordgren modestly does not note the fact that he himself has a small part in the latter, as Chief Constable of a local police district.)

Appendices

Top Twenty Nordic Noir Novels

(Taking The Girl with the Dragon Tattoo *as read, and in no particular order)*

Miss Smilla's Feeling for Snow (1992)
PETER HØEG
The atmospheric literary crime novel that almost single-handedly inaugurated – without trying to – the current Scandinavian invasion. *Miss Smilla's Feeling for Snow* mesmerises with its evocative use of Copenhagen locales and weather, so significant for the troubled, intuitive heroine. Most of all, it's the poetic quality of the novel that haunts the reader.

The Laughing Policeman (1968)
MAJ SJÖWALL AND PER WAHLÖÖ
Two writers – a crime-writing team – might be said to have started it all. The critical stock of Sjöwall/Wahlöö could not be higher: they are celebrated as the very best exponents of the police procedural. Martin Beck is the ultimate Scandinavian copper, and if you prefer to ignore the subtle Marxist perspective of the books, it is easy to do so.

Last Rituals (2005)
YRSA SIGURÐARDÓTTIR
Gruesome but compelling Scandicrime (eye gougings and strangulation) in the Icelandic Yrsa Sigurdardóttir's typically uncompromising style.

The Redbreast (2000)
JO NESBO

Jo Nesbo is certainly *the* breakthrough Nordic crime writer post-Larsson, and more quirky and individual than most of his Scandinavian colleagues – not least thanks to Nesbo's wonderfully dyspeptic detective Harry Hole (pronounced 'Hurler'). *The Redbreast* bristles with a terrifying vision of Nordic fascism.

Mercy (2008)
JUSSI ADLER-OLSEN

Scarifying fare set against a dark and vividly realised Copenhagen (where he was born) from an uncompromising writer who is breaking big in Britain.

1222 (2010)
ANNE HOLT

As ex-minister of justice for her country, Holt hardly paints a roseate picture of Norway's urban areas and outer reaches; *1222* has a classic, isolated setting for its mayhem: a frigid Finse.

Firewall (1998)
HENNING MANKELL

Mankell's Kurt Wallander is one of the great creations of modern crime fiction: overweight, diabetes-ridden and with all the problems of modern society leaving scars on his soul. *Firewall* is one of the writer's unvarnished portraits of modern life, in which society and all its institutions (not least the family) are put under the microscope.

Echoes from the Dead (2007)
JOHAN THEORIN

A windswept, isolated island on which the legacy of the past hangs heavy – at least in the disturbing novels of Johan Theorin. There is no Scandinavian writer more adept at conjuring unease than the disturbing, poetic Theorin; this is one of his signature books.

He Who Fears the Wolf (2003)
KARIN FOSSUM

Norway's Ruth Rendell, Karin Fossum, with more acute psychological insight than to be found in many a more respectable 'literary' novel.

Woman with Birthmark (1996)
HÅKAN NESSER

Where does Håkan Nesser set his novels? It's not important; his crime fiction, located in an unnamed Scandinavian country, is so commandingly written it makes most contemporary crime fare seem rather thin gruel. Nesser's copper, Van Veeteren, has been lauded by Colin Dexter.

The Consorts of Death (2009)
GUNNAR STAALESEN

Master of the Scandi private eye novel, Gunnar Staalesen (and Norwegian heir apparent of Ross Macdonald), on cracking form.

Jar City (2000)
ARNALDUR INDRIĐASON

The talented Indridason has made his mark as The King of the Icelandic Thriller with his Reykjavik-set thrillers. His debut, *Jar City* (successfully filmed), is Indridason's calling card. When the body of an old man is found in his apartment, DI Erlendur discovers that the murdered man has been accused of rape in the past.

The Ice Princess (2002)
CAMILLA LÄCKBERG

Agatha Christie's St Mary Mead transported to Sweden, courtesy of the Swedish Mistress of Menace – with added bloodshed.

The Blinded Man/Misterioso (1999)
ARNE DAHL

The inaugural book in Dahl's 'Intercrime' sequence has enjoyed much favourable attention; it's ambitious, complex and taut.

The Priest of Evil (2003)
MATTI JOENSUU
Helsinki is perhaps less frequented than other Scandinavian crime spots, and the late Matti Joensuu is the perfect conduit to Finland's less welcoming alleys.

Easy Money (2010)
JENS LAPIDUS
According to the urbane crime writer-cum-lawyer Jens Lapidus, Stockholm is quite as violent and dangerous as any drug-ridden American city; this first book in a trilogy is something different (and on a larger canvas) than most Nordic Noir fare.

Cell 8 (2011)
ANDERS ROSLUND & BÖRGE HELLSTRÖM
It was at a criminal rehabilitation centre that this acerbic team of writers first encountered each other; their joint creation, Ewert Grens, is a Stockholm cop. Not for the faint-hearted.

Red Wolf (2003)
LIZA MARKLUND
A trip down the sinister streets of Luleå in the company of investigative reporter Annika Bengtzon may not be in the tourist board brochure, but you won't forget it.

The Savage Altar (2006)
ÅSA LARSSON
Lashings of atmosphere distinguish Larsson's uncompromising fiction, with Sweden's Kiruna her protagonist Rebecka Martinsson's bolthole.

The Last Fix (2000)
KO DAHL
Veteran Norwegian writer KO Dahl's novel, *The Last Fix*, though not his first, is a calling card book. Oslo detectives Frank Frølich and Inspector Gunnarstranda are notable Scandi coppers in a bustling arena.

TOP SIX NORDIC NOIR FILMS

(In no particular order)

JAR CITY (2006)
Though well received on its first appearance, *Jar City* did not perhaps make the impact that was its due (perhaps it arrived a little too early in the growing wave of interest in Scandinavian crime fiction films), but this solid and understated adaptation of Arnaldur Indriðason's signature novel has steadily accrued more followers over the years. The grim picture of Icelandic crime presented here (involving genetic disease and multiple murder) may not reflect the realities of Icelandic society, but makes for a compelling experience.

THE MILLENNIUM TRILOGY (2009)
Rather as the appearance of Kenneth Branagh's Wallander prompted an almost stock response – 'Ah, but the Swedish version was better!' – a similar syndrome seems to operate when comparing the original Swedish film of Larsson's *The Girl with the Dragon Tattoo* with the perfectly creditable David Fincher remake – in other words, the Swedish version (along with its two sequels, which are yet to have Hollywood equivalents) did better service to the novel. The main coinage utilised in this argument is the Lisbeth Salander of Noomi Rapace set against the slightly less abrasive incarnation of the computer hacker by Rooney Mara. Whatever your view, there is one ineluctable fact: the original Swedish film of the first Larsson novel is now the most profitable Swedish film ever made.

JO NESBO'S HEADHUNTERS (2011)
Ironically, the first film to appear in which Jo Nesbo's name is actually part of the title is not a version of one of his series featuring the saturnine Harry Hole, but a lively and kinetic standalone novel which is closer to the kind of blackly comic crime of films such as *A Simple Plan*. But prior to the appearance of any Harry Hole movies, *Jo Nesbo's Headhunters* will do nicely, with director Morten Tydlum sounding just the right sardonic note as the

bodycount rises. Hapless (and secretly criminal) corporate headhunter Roger Brown (played with a winningly seedy mixture of corruption and innocence by Aksel Hennie) makes a bad mistake when robbing one of his clients; a visit to an outdoor toilet will never seem the same.

INSOMNIA (1997)

We are back again to the argument mentioned above – the Scandinavian original was better. This dark and disturbing film was remade (effectively enough) by Christopher Nolan as a vehicle for Al Pacino, but in conveying the truly unsettling descent into psychosis of a driven and conflicted detective, Stellan Skarsgård is in a class of his own – and the key moral issues addressed by the film are examined with greater rigour in this first film of *Insomnia*.

PUSHER (1996)

We are now familiar with Kim Bodnia as the sympathetic, up-against-it Danish copper of *The Bridge*, but a glance at his abrasive first film of *Pusher* (prior to its 2012 American remake), is a reminder of what a versatile actor he is – and how (like the very best of his profession) Bodnia is not concerned with presenting a series of admirable characters. The desperate drug pusher Frank at the centre of this uncompromising tale is a memorably etched protagonist, and it's hardly surprising that the Danish director Nicolas Winding Refn was able to use the film as a kind of calling card for the successful Hollywood career he is now enjoying.

THE HUNTERS (1996)

As the actor Rolf Lassgård becomes ever more familiar to British audiences for his succession of conflicted sleuths and related characters, it is perhaps time for audiences to reacquaint themselves with one of his biggest commercial successes, a film which enjoyed almost unprecedented success in its native Sweden and other territories. What makes this lean and effective thriller function effectively is the contrast between the Arcadian landscapes we are shown and the dark psychological conflicts played out against this beautiful backdrop. The success of the film has led to a belated sequel, *False Trails*.

TOP SIX NORDIC NOIR TV DRAMAS

(In no particular order)

WALLANDER (Sweden, UK)

Let's face it, whichever of the three very different TV series (two Swedish, one British) is your own particular favourite, Henning Mankell aficionados have cause to be grateful that considerable justice has been done to his work in these various adaptations – and the fact that some of the Mankell books have been filmed more than once makes for fascinating comparisons (with tricky political aspects, unsurprisingly, more pronounced in the Swedish series). And with three equally different actors playing Wallander, viewers are given plenty of ammunition for arguments as to which comes closest to Mankell's dyspeptic original.

THE KILLING (Denmark)

The makers of the cult Danish crime series (including its estimable producer, Piv Bernth, now Head of Drama at the originating company DR) were – to put it mildly – taken by surprise at the enthusiastic British embrace of the series; apart from the show's success in its native Denmark, Britain (of all nations in the world) took the difficult, tenacious Sarah Lund (Faroe Island jumper and all) to their collective hearts. Not so American viewers, who were not prepared to read those challenging subtitles (some, even, with two-syllable words) and who made their own controversially received English-language version, subsequently cancelled.

THE BRIDGE (Sweden, Denmark)

The Killing was always going to be a difficult act to follow, but that knotty trick was pulled off with aplomb by this remarkably successful series, with actress Sofia Helin allowing her unpolished autistic copper, Saga Norén, to demonstrate even fewer people skills than Lisbeth Salander and Sarah Lund combined. But don't overlook the contribution of Kim Bodnia, playing the Danish copper with a problematic family and a penchant for ill-advised extra-marital affairs – it's through his amazed eyes that we view the outrageous behaviour of Saga.

BORGEN (Denmark)
Initially conceived as a political drama, this mesmerising and multi-layered Danish show also takes on board all the accoutrements of the political thriller (à la *All the President's Men*), with a bustling variety of revelations involving parliamentary double-dealing and backstabbing – which turn out to be as compelling as anything more murderous in *The Killing*. *Borgen's* treatment of both politics and the dynamics of a marriage is more sophisticated than most viewers had seen from Britain and America.

SEBASTIAN BERGMAN (Sweden)
A bleak, intelligent show benefiting immensely from the presence of the bear-like Rolf Lassgård, but not quite overcoming two problematical aspects: the unsympathetic nature of its sex-pest hero and the derivative nature of some of the plots (Thomas Harris is liberally sampled).

VARG VEUM (Norway)
When the much-respected Norwegian film company SF Norge announced a series of films based on Gunnar Staalesen's much-acclaimed private eye novels, fingers were crossed hopefully. The first film, *Bitter Flowers*, had a highly successful cinema showing before its TV incarnation, inaugurating a solid and ambitious series. As Staalesen's sleuth, the Norwegian actor Trond Espen Seim – while too pretty in Brad Pitt fashion – was a good casting choice as the eponymous Varg.

Index

Index